THE BOOK OF
COLOR

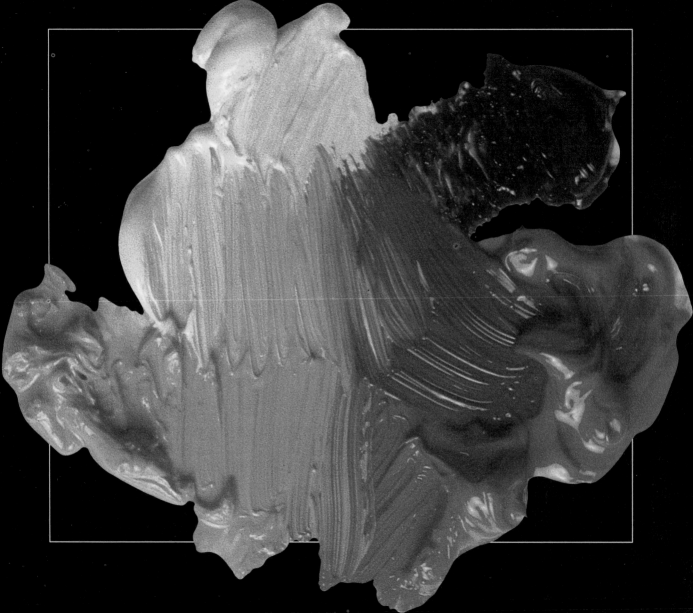

THE BOOK OF COLOR

by José M. Parramón

The history of color,
color theory, and contrast;
the color of forms and shadows;
color ranges and mixes;
and the practice of painting
with color

WATSON – GUPTILL PUBLICATIONS / NEW YORK

First published in the United States
by Watson-Guptill Publications,
a division of BPI Communications, Inc.,
1515 Broadway, New York, New York 10036.

Library of Congress Cataloging-in-Publication Data

Parramón, José María.
    [Gran libro del color. English]
    The book of color: the history of color, color theory,
  and contrast; the color of forms and shadows; color ranges and mixes;
  and the practice of painting with color/José M. Parramón.
      p.   cm.
    Includes bibliographical references.
    ISBN 0-8230-0516-X
    1. Color in art. 2. Color—History. I. Title.
ND1488.P3513 1993
752—dc20   92-38381
                                      CIP

Manufactured in Spain

1 2 3 4 5 6 7 8 9 10/02 01 00 99 98 97 96 95 94 93

Contents

Fig. 1. José M. Parramón (1919-   ),
*Urban Landscape: Plaza San Agustín,
Barcelona*. Private collection.

To my brother Luis, priest and doctor
of Philosophy and History

Contents

Fig. 2. José M. Parramón (1919–   ),
Landscape of Ravenna, Italy. Private
collection.

3

3A

Fig. 3. José M. Parramón (1919–   ), *San Miguel Bathhouse, Barcelona*. Private collection.

Fig. 3A. It is important to begin drawing and painting by preparing several sketches in order to determine the basic structure, color, and composition of the subject.

Introduction

Until the mid-nineteenth century artists all over the world painted their pictures without directly observing nature. As a result, they imagined and created landscapes for the backgrounds of their paintings and resolved the color of shadows with drab, brownish pigments such as *burnt umber* and *bitumen of Judea*, colors that frequently were used for this purpose throughout the eighteenth and into the nineteenth century.

In 1850 a group of young French painters, who would thirty years later be called *Impressionists*, left their studios for the forests of Barbizon to paint in the open air. They quickly noticed three basic aspects of color: that the color of the shadows was not bitumen of Judea, but complemented the color of the light; that blue is present in all shadows ("I am continually looking for blue," said van Gogh); and that nature is light and color.

Since then, color has become an overwhelmingly important element in a painting, to such an extent that pictures are painted with nothing but color. Pierre Bonnard, the renowned painter who founded the *Nabis*, who later became an *Intimist* and finally a *colorist*, wrote, "Color can express everything without having to revert to relief or the model."

The power of color in painting is clear, so we must understand it. We must study color theory—including the discoveries of Newton, Young, Maxwell, and Hertz—to understand that with only three colors we can produce all the colors that exist in nature. We must know which they are, how their complements are used, and what color contrast, the range of contrasts, and simultaneous contrasts are. While gathering information about and studying color theory for this book in order to summarize it and make it accessible to students, I encountered a few surprises. For example, many texts I reviewed refer to a spectrum of seven colors when, in

fact, television, photography, and the graphic arts have proven through the processes of *additive synthesis* and *subtractive synthesis* that there are only three *primary colors* and three *secondary colors*, a total of *six*. Therefore, a spectrum of seven colors cannot possibly exist.

But the problems of color are not only theoretical. During the years in which Monet was painting his famous series, *Water Lilies*, at the lake in his garden in Giverny, he wrote in a letter to Gustave Geffroy: "There are colors that seem impossible. For example, the color of the weeds that move at the bottom of a lake. It's enough to drive you crazy when you try to paint it." But Monet finally managed to paint the weeds, because he was aware of the factors that determine the color of forms. He knew exactly which colors he had to mix in order to compose the color of the weeds under the water. In a phrase, he knew how to solve the *practical problems* of color.

Eighty pages of text with more than four hundred color illustrations give you the practical methods of color usage. Beginning with a study of the local and tonal color of objects, the book then proceeds to a discussion of contrast and atmosphere, the use and abuse of black and white, and what colors should be mixed when resolving the color of shadows. The text continues with a study of the composition of colors, including a look at color harmonization, followed by a study of mixing with two or three colors, then with all colors. Finally, to put all of the above into practice, several professional artists will each paint a subject in which color is the basic element, using oil, watercolor, and pastel.

I have devoted the first pages of this book to the history of color, a summary of the techniques, facts, and artists who contributed to the evolution of color and created new ways and styles of painting. From the prehistoric era to Picasso, this section

4

covers the Egyptians, the Greeks, Giotto, van Eyck, Caravaggio, Rubens, and Velázquez, up through the Impressionists, Manet, Monet, Cézanne, and Picasso.

I hope the paintings, the text, and the hundreds of images that illustrate this book will inspire you to paint with color, seeing your subject as one of the great masters would have. According to Picasso, Cézanne "painted without stopping at a particular part of the picture, always studying the reflection of colors and everything that appeared around them."

José M. Parramón

Fig. 4. José M. Parramón, author of this book, artist, painter, and art educator, has written more than thirty-five books on art instruction, which have been translated and published in twelve languages.

5

6

7

Thirty thousand years ago Paleolithic artists painted with only two colors, yellow ocher and sepia red, as well as black and white; 25,000 years later, the Egyptians developed pigments for blue and green. During the eighth century A.D. the Phoenicians discovered the famous Tyrian purple; around the same time, the scribes of medieval Europe invented the invaluable ultramarine blue. In time, more colors were discovered or invented, and by the eighteenth century there were 30,000 shades available to painters, dyers, and weavers. In 1980 the number of commercially produced colors had risen to 90,000. This remarkable rate of development promoted the invention of new media and painting techniques, generating controversy, change, and divergent styles: the history of color in the art of painting.

THE HISTORICAL EVOLUTION OF COLOR

8

9

Prehistoric artists (30000 B.C.)

10

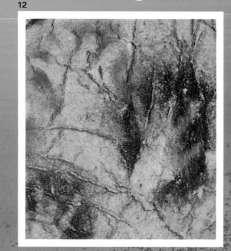

11

12

At the beginning of the twentieth century in the Austrian village of Willendorf, a small statue of a female with enormous breasts and exaggerated buttocks was found (fig. 11). This strange figure, today known as the *Venus of Willendorf*, was attributed to prehistoric artists of the *Aurignacian* period. In the 1960s the Venus of Willendorf was carbon dated at 29,880 years old. Two other remarkable pieces of Paleolithic art are the hands in negative in the cavern at Gargas in the High Pyrenees (fig. 12), painted 29,200 years ago, and the cave paintings of animals at Lascaux (Dordogne), France (fig. 10), which belongs to a more recent period, the Upper Paleolithic, dated at 13,500 years old. Before reviewing the materials and colors that prehistoric artists used, allow me to explain the technique of carbon dating, which makes it possible to determine the age of pre-

historic art and other found objects. While developing a method to determine the amount of *carbon 14* in the atmosphere, Frank Libby, an American and winner of the Nobel Prize for Chemistry, discovered that this radioactive isotope is continuously absorbed by humans, animals, and plants while living, and returns to the atmosphere after death at an extremely slow rate. With the aid of a Geiger counter, Libby learned that after a period of 5,700 years, the activity of carbon 14 is reduced by half; in this way, the age of an object or painting can be determined by the remaining amount.

Fig. 10. *Bull with Reindeer* (cave painting). Upper Paleolithic (c. 13,500 B.C.). Lascaux, Dordogne (France). Prehistoric artists sometimes superimposed images; here we can see two red reindeer merged with a black bull.

The noted archaeologist Nougier commented that when Paleolithic artists began to sketch on soft clay more than 30,000 years ago, "they seemed to get drunk on their new invention." Less than a millenium later, primitive humans were painting silhouettes of hands, as well as negative handprints. The technique for the latter consisted of pressing the hand against a wall and blowing paint onto it through a piece of hollow cane or bone (fig. 15A).

About 15,000 to 20,000 years later, these paintings were discovered in caves at Altamira in northern Spain, and at Lascaux and La Mouthe in France, along with paintings of reindeer, goats, boar, horses, and mammoths. These early artists painted with six pigments diluted in animal fat, using bowls and palettes of stone and crude horsehair brushes.

Fig. 11. *Venus of Willendorf.* Aurignacian period (c. 29,880 B.C.). Natural History Museum, Vienna. The figure's large breasts and prominent buttocks were symbols of sexuality, fertility, and maternity.

Fig. 12. *Negative Handprint.* Aurignacian period (c. 29,880 B.C.). Cavern at Gargas (High Pyrenees). These outlines were made by pressing a hand against the cave wall and blowing paint onto it through a piece of hollow cane or bone.

Fig. 13. An artist's rendering depicting prehistoric artists painting on the walls of a cave.

Fig. 15. An assembly of some of the materials thought to be used by prehistoric artists.

13

14

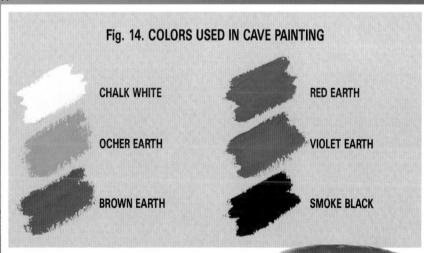

Fig. 14. COLORS USED IN CAVE PAINTING

CHALK WHITE   RED EARTH

OCHER EARTH   VIOLET EARTH

BROWN EARTH   SMOKE BLACK

15

A

The artists of ancient Egypt (3000 B.C.)

16

In ancient Egypt there were several gods of the dead. The most famous were Osiris and Anubis; the latter was depicted as a human being with the head of a jackal. As the god of embalmment he presided over burials and escorted immortal souls to the afterlife.

Because the Egyptians firmly believed that the soul would reunite with the body after death, they tried to prevent the deterioration of the corpse by mummifying it. They also painted pictures of the deceased and scenes from his or her life and personal belongings on the walls of the tomb so that the person could continue to enjoy them in the hereafter, and to facilitate the meeting of body and soul.

Fig. 16. *The Queen in Adoration*. Tomb of Nofretete, Valley of the Kings. Tebas, Egypt.

Fig. 17. *Funerary Portrait*. Mid-eleventh century A.D. Staliche Museum, Berlin.

Fig. 18. *Funeral Offerings*. Tomb of Menna. Tebas, Egypt.

17

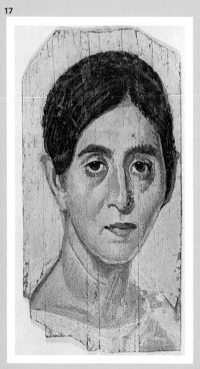

18

Some art historians believe that the Egyptians invented the art of drawing by outlining profiles cast from shadows made by the sun. It is true that the figures represented in ancient Egyptian wall drawings and paintings always appear with the head and legs in profile and the torso in a frontal position. The men were painted with a dark ocher or sienna and the women with a light ocher or yellow, with the hair and eyes always in black. The artists had seven colors available to them: yellow, ocher, sienna, red, green, blue, and violet (as well as black and white, with which they composed gray). They also produced the first inorganic synthetic pigments: *blue frit*, a clear, glasslike blue, and *lead white*, which is still used today. For utensils, they used shells as palettes, pots and jars made of baked clay, and brushes of palm fiber or chewed cane. They worked in teams and sometimes erected scaffolding to paint large murals.

Fig. 19. An artist's rendering showing ancient Egyptian artists planning the composition and painting the walls of a tomb.

Fig. 21. A selection of pigments and equipment used by the artists of ancient Egypt.

19

20

Fig. 20. COLORS USED BY ANCIENT EGYPTIAN ARTISTS

LEAD WHITE	RED EARTH
GRAY	MALACHITE GREEN
DARK YELLOW	EGYPTIAN BLUE
BURNT UMBER	VIOLET EARTH
BROWN EARTH	SMOKE BLACK

21

Polygnotus, Apelles, and Zeuxis (500 B.C.)

The chronicles of ancient Greek art tell us that Polygnotus, founder of a school of art in Athens, was one of the great masters of mural painting in Delphi; they speak of how Alexander the Great chose Apelles as his private portrait artist; they comment on the realism of Zeuxis's paintings, which attracted birds to the grapes he had depicted.

Unfortunately, there are no surviving works of these great masters, though their artistic prowess is reflected in the copies that were often drawn on ceramics (figs. 23 and 24). It is also known that most of the mural paintings found in the ruins of Pompeii and Herculaneum are copies of Greek paintings, which, in spite of their imperfections, are proof of the high artistic level reached by ancient Greek painters (fig. 25).

According to Pliny, Latin historian of the first century B.C., "With only four colors, white, ocher, red, and black, the great painters, Apelles, Aischion, Melanthius, and Nicómaco, created immortal works whose value was comparable with all the riches of a city." But the Greeks also painted with Naples yellow, sepia, and red, in addition to green and blue. Under Roman rule, Tyrian purple, obtained from the mollusk murex, was added to the artist's palette. The Greeks painted in *fresco*, a medium we will discuss later in this book. Another style commonly used by the Greeks was *encaustic wax*, a procedure in which pigment was mixed with beeswax. After heating, the colored wax was applied with a brush and a utensil known as a *cestrum*, which is similar to a spatula. An example of this type of painting can be seen on page 14 (fig. 17) in a portrait of a mummy of Fayum, a province of Egypt, attributed to Greek artists of the mid-eleventh century A.D.

Fig. 23. *Greek Amphora*. Second century B.C. Archaeological Museum of Catalonia, Barcelona.

Fig. 24. *Perfume Jar*. Fragment of an illustration in which the use of green can still be seen. National Museum, Athens.

Fig. 22. COLORS USED BY GREEK AND ROMAN ARTISTS

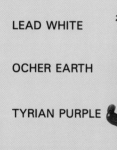

22
LEAD WHITE

OCHER EARTH

TYRIAN PURPLE

SMOKE BLACK

NAPLES YELLOW

ROYAL YELLOW

BROWN EARTH

GRAY

GREEK GREEN (VERDIGRIS)

MALACHITE BLUE

23

24

25

Manuscript illumination

During the sixth and seventh centuries A.D. the history of art was stalled for two reasons. First, all figurative representation was prohibited by the *iconoclastic movement*, which was promoted by the Church in an effort to combat the sensualism of the Classical period. Second, the barbarian invasion caused the flight of both king and commoner from the city to the country. According to Arnold Hauser in his *Social History of Art*, it was a time when "nobody was capable of painting a human figure." Fortunately, this dark period ended in the eighth century when Charlemagne, king of the Franks and emperor of the West, named the most prominent intellectuals in Western culture as ministers of his court. The most famous was the Anglo-Saxon monk Alcuin of York, who established several abbey schools or *scriptoria*. Among several other techniques, manuscript illumination, an art that was practiced until the nineteenth century, was studied.

The artists who decorated these manuscripts developed four important colors: ultramarine blue (derived from lapis lazuli), yellow orpiment (from arsenic and sulfur), red (from lead), and verdigris (from copper acetate). They painted with watercolors, using oxhair brushes and quills on vellum or parchment.

Fig. 25. (Opposite page) *Hercules and Telephui*. Herculean Temple. Fresco painting from the Roman period, copied from a Greek painting of the fourth century B.C.

Fig. 26. The Limbourg Brothers. A page from the *Très Riches Heures du Duc de Berry*.

Fig. 27. Disciple of Quentin Massys (c. 1465–1530), *Saint Luke Painting the Virgin and Child*. The National Gallery, London.

Fig. 28. COLORS USED FOR MANUSCRIPT ILLUMINATION

ULTRAMARINE BLUE
Made from *lapis lazuli*, a semi-precious stone, it was first used around the eighth century A.D.

ORPIMENT YELLOW
Derived from sulfur and arsenic, it was used by the Egyptians, who called it *royal gold*.

RUBY RED
Medieval scribes called it "Dragon's Blood."

VERDIGRIS
Made from copper acetate by the Greeks and Romans, it was used until the nineteenth century.

The first realist: Giotto (1276–1337)

"... He became so good at imitating nature that he did away with the rough style of Byzantine art and revived realism and the good art of painting."

This quotation, from the *Lives of the Artists* by Giorgio Vasari (1568), describes Giotto's life. According to Vasari's account, Giotto was born in Vespignano, near Florence.

"One day," writes Vasari, "when the great master and artist Cimabue was going to Florence, he crossed paths with the child Giotto, who was then ten years old. Cimabue was amazed to see the astonishing realism with which Giotto painted a flock of sheep, using a flat stone as his support. Cimabue asked Giotto if he would like to learn how to paint. When Cimabue received his father's permission they set off for Florence." Twenty years later, Dante Alighieri, Cimabue's contemporary and a friend of Giotto's, wrote in his *Divine Comedy:*

I considered Cimabue to be the best painter.
But it is Giotto who predominates today and Cimabue's fame is now obscured.

Giotto is considered to be the founder of modern painting due to his use of realism and naturalism. His style influenced almost all of the painters of the fourteenth century, including Masaccio and, later on, Michelangelo.

Fig. 29. Giotto (1276–1337), *The Crucifixion*. Chapel of the Scrovegni, Padua. Along with his master Cimabue, Giotto is considered to be one of the founders of modern painting, introducing an imaginative and passionate naturalism into his work.

Fig. 30. Giotto, *The Cry Before the Death of Christ*. Chapel of the Scrovegni, Padua. Note Giotto's characteristic use of emotion in the angel's expression, reflected in both its face and its gesture.

29

30

31

Fig. 31. Here we can see the *zones of interruption* and *union* of a fresco, which correspond to the image in figure 29.

Figs. 32 to 35. (Opposite page) In these four images we can see how egg tempera is made by mixing powdered pigment with a liquid made of one fresh egg yolk and an equal part of distilled water.

Egg tempera

Giotto painted most of his works in *fresco* (a technique we will look more closely at on the next page), but sometimes he painted in egg tempera. This technique involves mixing powdered pigments with a liquid made from one fresh egg yolk and an equal part of distilled water.

Refer to the materials and color preparation in figures 32 to 35. First, the yolk is separated from the white (fig. 32), then put into a pot (fig. 33). Next, the distilled water is added (fig. 34). The mixture is shaken, then combined with a powdered pigment and stirred with a spatula (fig. 35). Once prepared, the mixture is stored in jars until needed. The technique is similar to tempera or *gouache*, allowing the artist to apply thick coats of glossy color, either opaque or transparent, depending on the density of the paint.

Fig. 36. Giotto, *Saint Stephen*. Horne Museum, Florence. Egg tempera on a golden background with touches of gold leaf on the saint's tunic.

Fig. 37. (Bottom of page) The materials needed for making egg tempera paint: (A) powdered pigment, (B) an egg yolk combined with an equal amount of water, (C) a marble or stone surface for mixing the pigment with the water and yolk solution, (D) a pestle for grinding the colors, (E) a spatula, and (F) hog's hair and sable brushes.

32 33 34 35 36 37

A C D E F B

Fresco painting

The technique of *buon fresco* (as the Italians called it) or *true fresco* consisted of painting directly on damp plaster that had been applied to a wall by the artist so that the fine, earth-toned colors used would be absorbed by the plaster and become part of the wall.

Fresco painting was already being practiced by Byzantine artists in the Romanesque murals of the Middle Ages, but it reached the height of its splendor during the Renaissance. All the great masters, from Giotto to Raphael and Michelangelo, painted murals in fresco. The most famous are Raphael's *Le Stanze*, and the ceiling of the Sistine Chapel by Michelangelo, both of which are in the Vatican.

Figs. 38 to 43. The procedure for painting in fresco: First, the wall is *plastered* with a coating of lime and sand (fig. 38), then a second coat is applied (39); following this, a wooden float is used to smooth the surface (40). Having previously determined the zones of interruption and union, the outline

of the drawing, done on thick paper, is gone over with a perforating wheel (41 and 41A); the image is then transferred onto the wall by gently tapping the outline with black pigment powder (42); to finish, the outlined image is painted in fresco, while the plaster is still damp.

Fig. 44. The following items, which are also used by masons, are indispensable for painting in fresco: (A) a bucket of sand, (B) a bucket of lime, (C) a container for mixing the plaster, (D) a float for applying the lime, (E) a mortarboard, (F) a trowel, (G) a level float for smoothing, (H) a tin of water for wetting the walls surface, (I) a brush to gradate colors (a sponge is better), (J) rags, (K) fine earth or powdered colors, (L) a palette, and (M) brushes.

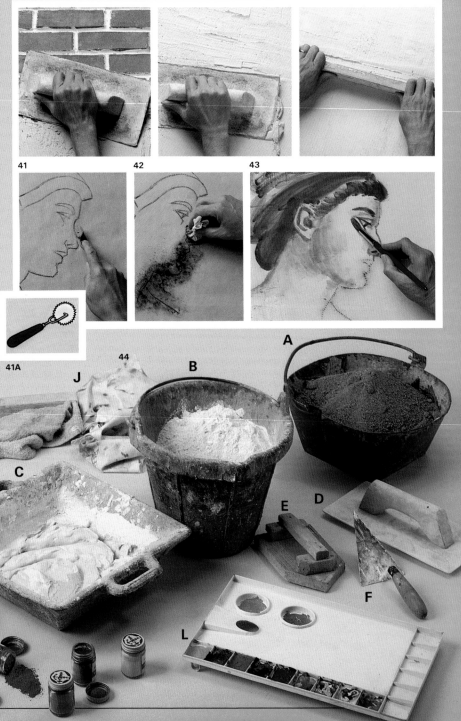

38 39 40

41 41A 42 43

44

A B C D E F G H I J K L M

Van Eyck (1390–1441) invents oil painting

Painting with oil and varnish seems to have first been done by the Chinese during the first centuries A.D., but the technique did not reach the West until the beginning of the fifteenth century. In 1410 in the city of Bruges, a young painter named Jan van Eyck discovered a formula that allowed oil colors to dry without difficulty. After setting out a painting in tempera treated with oils to dry in the sun, the picture not only dried but cracked. Van Eyck then decided to look for a varnish that would dry in the shade. In his *Lives* Vasari writes, ''After carrying out many different and varied mixes, Giovanni [Jan] discovered that linseed oil boiled with 'white Bruges varnish'

produced the desired effect. He found that when the colors dried they were not only resistant but when left at the mercy of the elements kept their intense shines without any application of varnish.''

In the year that van Eyck was born (1390), the Florentine painter Cennino Cennini wrote his famous *Il Libro dell'arte (The Craftsman's Handbook)*, from which we may learn about the techniques, materials, and colors that were used by the artists of his time. From ancient Greece to the Renaissance the number and quality of colors increased considerably. Cennini mentions eighteen colors, as well as five blacks and two whites (see fig. 46).

Fig. 45. Jan van Eyck (1390–1441), *Wedding Portrait*. The National Gallery, London. One of the first pictures to be painted in oil, thanks to van Eyck's experimentation.

Fig. 46. According to *The Craftsman's Handbook* (1390) by Cennino Cennini, the following is the range of colors that were used by artists from the fourteenth century onward.

45

46

RENAISSANCE COLORS

SILVER WHITE

NAPLES YELLOW

ROYAL YELLOW

YELLOW OCHER

NATURAL SIENNA

DARK SEPIA

VERMILION

RED LAKE

TYRIAN PURPLE

MALACHITE GREEN

VERDIGRIS

EARTH GREEN

EGYPTIAN BLUE

ULTRAMARINE BLUE

VIOLET

SMOKE BLACK

Masters of the Renaissance: Leonardo da Vinci (1452–1519)

Born in Vinci, a province of Florence, Leonardo, a peasant, was the illegitimate son of a notary. At the age of seventeen he became an apprentice in the studio of Verrocchio; by the age of twenty he had already become a master of the Guild.

In addition to being a painter, sculptor, and architect, Leonardo investigated and established the fundamentals of anatomy, aeronautics, and the human circulatory system, designed weapons, studied atmospheric physics, and drafted the notes that would later be published as his *Treatise of Painting*.

Through his creative ability and technical skill, Leonardo contributed to the development and splendor of the art of the High Renaissance of the sixteenth century, surpassing, in Vasari's words, the "dry and hard style" of the *Quattrocento*, which included the work of Masaccio, Ucello, Fra Angelico, and others previously considered to be masters. Leonardo achieved this by employing the technique of *sfumato*, which he himself summarized and defined as follows: "Try to be delicate with your figures instead of concentrating on shaping them clearly with a dry technique. . . . Note how shadows and light are joined not by lines but by something close to a cloud of smoke." A notable example of *sfumato* can be seen in Leonardo's famous painting the *Mona Lisa*, or *La Gioconda* (see fig. 48).

As much in his paintings as in his *Treatise of Painting*, Leonardo developed the rules of *aerial perspective*, which he defined as "the great distance between the eye and the mountains, by which they appear to be blue, almost the color of air; the fields also participate in the blue the farther they are from the eye." He also determined "that you will have to finish the foreground clearly and precisely; and do the same for the middle distance but in a more vaporous style, more confused or, better said, less precise, and continue successively according to the distances . . . with distance the contours become less hard and the shapes and colors will gradually disappear." Leonardo also dictated rules of color: "The white, from the sun and the air in the open air, has bluish shadows. So white is not a color but the result of other colors."

47

48

Michelangelo (1475–1564) and Raphael (1483–1520)

Surprise! The Sistine Chapel is not the same—Michelangelo's colors have changed. As a result of the restoration sponsored in the late 1980s by NTV, the Japanese Television Network Corporation, we now know that Michelangelo's palette included light, lustrous, luminous colors that bear no relation to the brownish hues that once covered his 314 figures (figs. 49 and 50).

There is really no need to be surprised, though: Since Michelangelo completed the Sistine Ceiling in 1512, and Edison invented the electric light in 1878, Michelangelo's work had been darkened by 360 years of smoke from the chapel's oil lamps.

In addition to painting the most celebrated mural in Western art, Michelangelo also created the most famous sculptures of the Renaissance: the *Pietà*, the *David*, and the *Moses*. The dome of St. Peter's in the Vatican, among many other building projects, proved him to be one of the greatest architects. Michelangelo was the archetypal "Renaissance man," a true genius. Raphael's is another story, no less thrilling. By the age of eighteen he had already painted *The Crucifixion of Two Saints* and *The Coronation of the Virgin*. In figure 51 you can see the *Madonna del Granduca*, painted by Raphael when he was twenty-one. By the age of twenty-six, he was already as famous and important as Michelangelo. It was then that Pope Julius II commissioned him to paint the *Le Stanze* in the Vatican Palace, where Michelangelo was painting the Sistine Ceiling. Unfortunately he died young, at the age of thirty-seven.

Figs. 47 and 48. Leonardo da Vinci (1452–1519), *The Virgin of the Rocks* and *La Gioconda*. The Louvre, Paris. Both paintings, particularly the latter, are good examples of *sfumato*, and of Leonardo's use of aerial perspective.

Figs. 49 and 50. Michelangelo (1475–1564), *The Delphic Sybil*, detail of the Sistine Ceiling. The Vatican. Here you can see one of the Sistine Chapel's paintings before (inset) and after (fig. 49) the restoration, which was carried out by a Vatican team of art conservators and sponsored by the Japanese Television Network Corporation.

Fig. 51. Raphael (1483–1520), *Madonna del Granduca*. Pitti Palace, Florence.

49

50

51

Modern painting: Titian (c. 1488–1576)

When Titian was ten years old his parents sent him to Venice with his uncle. Seeing the young boy's desire to become a painter, Titian's uncle apprenticed him to the studio of Giovanni Bellini, the most famous painter in Venice at that time. History tells us that Titian learned from Bellini "the experiences and disciplines of drawing, the synthesis of perspective, and the practice of form and color."

While Titian was a teenager, another of Bellini's apprentices, Giorgione, was achieving great success. Vasari described him thus: "He painted directly, because Giorgione believed that painting without a drawing was the true and best way of painting." Titian was fascinated by Giorgione's use of color and so strongly influenced by him that several of Titian's works were later attributed to Giorgione, and vice versa. In 1510 the plague invaded Venice, and Giorgione was one of millions who died in the epidemic. Ten years later, having completed dozens of famous paintings, such as *Sacred Love* and *Profane Love*, Titian became the one of the most important painters of the

Renaissance, along with Raphael and Michelangelo.

By the age of sixty, the old master had developed a freer and more spontaneous style (see figs. 54 and 55), which provoked criticism from other artists. Michelangelo commented: "It's a pity that in Venice they don't start off learning how to draw properly." However, Vasari was of the opinion that "Titian's style in his latest works is very different from that when he was young. His first works were painted with an extreme fineness to be observed from close up, whereas the last ones, applied with rough half-impastos and color staining, cannot be observed from close up . . . but seen from afar appear to be perfect in all ways. And such a procedure is admirable because it brings the painting to life."

Clearly, Venice and Titian foresaw modern painting.

Fig. 52. Titian (1488–1576), *Self-portrait*. The Prado, Madrid.

Fig. 53. Titian, *Presentation of Mary at the Temple*. Academy Galleries, Venice.

52

Figs. 54 and 55. Titian, *Christ Crowned with Thorns* (with an enlarged detail). Pinakothek, Munich. Note in the detail the spontaneous workmanship, resolved with loose brush work and *frottage*.

Fig. 56. Titian, *Danäe Receiving the Rain of Gold*. The Prado, Madrid. As in all of Titian's work, we can see that his painting is a clear expression of vision and a mastery of color. His use of *frottage* was later employed and copied by such great masters as Rubens, Velázquez, and Rembrandt.

53

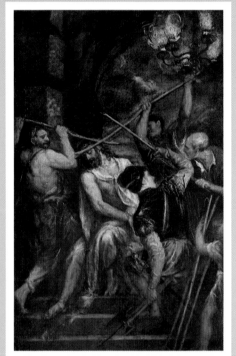

Caravaggio's use of light and shadow (1573–1610)

Born Michelangelo Merisi in the village of Caravaggio, at the age of ten the future artist was orphaned and went to work as an apprentice in the studio of Simone Peterzano in Milan. It was there that his fellow apprentices named him Caravaggio. At age eighteen he traveled to Rome to work for another artist; the people and atmosphere he encountered in the taverns and barrooms that appeared as subjects in his work were always portrayed in intense contrasts of color, light, and shadow, which defined his painting as *Tenebrist*. But his style transformed *Baroque* painting and influenced the work of the greatest artists of the *Cinquecento*, from Velázquez to Rembrandt, Rubens to La Tour, as well as Ribera, Zurbarán, Le Nain, Jordaens, Vermeer, and many others.

Fig. 57. Caravaggio (1573–1610), *The Conversion of Saint Paul*. Santa Maria del Popolo, Rome. One example of Caravaggio's *Tenebrism*.

Fig. 58. Caravaggio, *David with the Head of Goliath* (detail). Borghese Gallery, Rome.

57

58

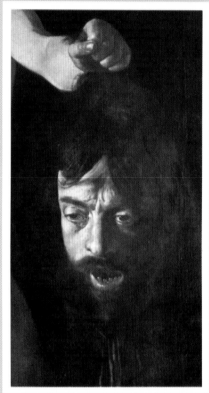

59

The classicism of Poussin (1594–1666)

The French painter Nicolas Poussin is considered to be the greatest representative of seventeeth-century French classicism. However, all of his work—except for six pictures he painted in Paris—was conceived and painted in Rome, where he married and lived for forty years.

At the beginning of his career he was a great admirer of Titian and Raphael, whom he imitated insatiably. With equal passion he despised Caravaggio as "an evildoer born to ruin painting."

Curiously, when Poussin needed to study composition, light, color, and the gestures of his figures, he constructed a small scene using wax dolls. A classical painter in both style and theme, Poussin alternated his work as an artist with reading the classics or visiting many ancient Roman monuments and buildings, which he depicted in his paintings of pagan gods and myths; *Venus and Adonis* (fig. 61) is one good example. Poussin also painted religious themes, such as the one shown in figure 60.

60

Fig. 59. Velázquez (1599–1660), *The Adoration of the Wise Kings* (detail). The Prado, Madrid. As you can see from this detail, in his youth Velázquez was heavily influenced by Caravaggio's use of contrast.

Figs. 60 and 61. Nicolas Poussin (1594–1666), *Saint Cecelia*, The Prado, Madrid; *Venus and Adonis*, Kimbell Art Museum, Fort Worth, Texas. Note Poussin's choice of subject, composition, and modeling, and his extremely classical approach.

61

The colorism of Rubens (1579–1640)

In 1987 Madrid's Prado Museum organized an exhibition of Rubens's paintings on loan from the National Museum of Stockholm, entitled "Rubens: Titian's Imitator."

During his life, Rubens copied paintings by Leonardo, Raphael, Correggio, Caravaggio, Giulio Romano, and others, demonstrating a certain predilection for the Venetians: Veronese, Tintoretto, and Titian. Having copied thirty of his paintings, why was Rubens so enamored of Titian's work? Rubens adopted from Titian and the other Venetians their intense chromatic scale and their vision of color or *colorism*. The assistant director of the Prado, Manuela Mena, confirmed this by saying that the Madrid exhibition allowed the public to appreciate "Rubens's interest in mainly seeing and studying the feeling of color, technique, sensuality, and freedom of expression."

In his lifetime, Rubens painted more than 2,500 pictures. His work method consisted of personally drawing small sketches, which he then passed on to assistants or disciples, who included such illustrious artists as Van Dyck, Jordaens, Snyders, Teniers, Brueghel de Velours, and Pane de Vos, with teams of experts working on several paintings at a time. It was previously believed that Rubens only executed sketches and added finishing touches to some of the paintings, but today it has been proven that Rubens, exploiting his creative powers and rich sense of color, was involved in all of his paintings from beginning to end.

Peter Paul Rubens won fame, fortune, honor, and prestige during his own lifetime. The government of the Netherlands appointed him to several diplomatic positions, giving him the opportunity to meet the aristocracy of Holland, Italy, France, Spain, and England. Above all, Rubens was a painter: the great colorist of Baroque art.

Fig. 62. Peter Paul Rubens (1579–1640), *The Fall of the Condemned*. Pinakothek, Munich. Rubens used a whirlwind of human forms to demonstrate his mastery of the nude and capture the color of the human body.

62

63

Figs. 63 and 64. Peter Paul Rubens, *The Horrors of War* (detail), Pitti Palace, Florence; *The Tiger and Lion Hunt*, Fine Arts Museum, Rennes. Two magnificent examples of Rubens's use of color and passionate dynamism, enhanced by the contrast of light and shadow and the wealth of color.

64

Pioneer of Impressionism: Velázquez (1599–1660)

Diego Rodríguez de Silva y Velázquez was born in Seville, Spain, in 1599. At the age of seventeen he was already recognized as a painter and had completed several noted pictures. At twenty he painted his first great picture, *The Adoration of the Wise Kings*. By the time he was twenty-four, word of the young artist had reached Madrid and King Philip IV named him Court Painter.

Thus began the career of one of the greatest masters of painting. In Madrid he had the chance to study in depth the Titians in the Spanish Royal Collection. Titian's vision and technique, his use of color, and loose brushwork transformed Velázquez's technique into his famous *manera abreviada*, or loose, quick style, making him a pioneer of Impressionism. One need only see the color, looseness, and finish of the jar of flowers (fig. 67), the gracefulness of the brush stroke in the weaver's blouse (fig. 66), the confident composition of the child's head painted *"alla prima"* (fig. 68), or the synthesis of the hand holding the flower (fig. 71) to realize that Velázquez's work set the standard for the Impressionists.

Édouard Manet, the founder of Impressionism, traveled to Madrid in 1785 and visited the Prado to copy some of Velázquez's paintings. In a letter to his friend and fellow painter Henri Fantin-Latour, Manet wrote: "How wonderful it is to see Velázquez's paintings. He is the Painter of painters. He has astonished me; he has captivated me."

Figs. 65 to 71. Velázquez (1599–1660). Most of the pictures on these pages are in the Prado, Madrid. *The Spinners*: The painting (fig. 65) and an enlarged detail (fig. 66) showing Velázquez's *manera abreviada*. Below left (fig. 67) is the vase of flowers in the *Infanta Margarita*, Kunsthistorisches Museum, Vienna. On the opposite page: *Prince Balthasar Carlos;* on the extreme right, *Philip IV;* below left, the *Infanta Margarita of Austria*, with an enlarged detail (fig. 71) of her hand holding a small bouquet of roses, an example of the artist's extraordinary pictorial synthesis.

65

66

67

68

69

70

71

Rembrandt (1606–1669) and chiaroscuro

Unlike other Dutch artists of his time, Rembrandt died without ever traveling to other countries. He was born in Leyden and lived there until he was twenty-five, when he moved to Amsterdam, where he died at age sixty-three. ''What do I want to go to Italy to see Leonardo or Titian for, if we have their paintings to study as much as we want here in the Netherlands?'' he said, although he was exposed indirectly to contemporary Italian influences. From the age of fifteen to eighteen he was apprenticed to two painters from Leyden who had worked in Italy. Later on in Amsterdam, he studied with Lastman, a painter who had also been in Italy and was a great enthusiast of Caravaggio.

During the early seventeenth century, Caravaggio had an enormous impact on the painters from Utrecht who were in Italy at that time. When they returned to Holland, their enthusiasm was such that they created the *Utrecht School*, based on Caravaggio's style. The Utrecht School promoted Caravaggism throughout Holland, influencing Hals, Vermeer, and Rembrandt.

It is very easy to see the influence of Caravaggio's Tenebrism on Rembrandt's technique of *chiaroscuro*, or an emphasis on the change from light to dark in a painting. If we compare the paintings done by Rembrandt during his youth to those he painted from the age of thirty onward, we can see how he progressively composed large parts of his pictures with dense shadows while at the same time emphasized the color and form of the figures.

To better understand Rembrandt's characteristic style, we need only look at figures 72 and 73. The center of interest is illuminated by direct light while the rest of the picture remains in partial shadow, with only enough light to distinguish the forms, causing notable contrasts similar to those in Caravaggio's work.

Figs. 72 and 73. Rembrandt (1606–1669), *The Sacred Family*, The Louvre, Paris; *The Adulteress*, the National Gallery, London. In both pictures we can see the use of *chiaroscuro*, or painting with light and shadow. Emphasizing his idea of chiaroscuro, Rembrandt highlighted the main subject, using contrast to tell the story.

72

73

Poussinistes and Rubénistes (1671–1672)

In 1671 there was a heated debate—the so-called *Quarrel of Color and Design*—between two factions in the Royal French Academy of Painting. One of the parties, the *Poussinistes*, considered drawing to be a fundamental element of painting, and supported their point of view with the perfect compositions and designs of works by Raphael, Carracci, and Poussin. The example of the latter, France's greatest classical painter (a point that the Poussinistes often used to inject a patriotic note into the discussion), was put forward to demonstrate an emphasis of form over color, suggesting that design and composition were of primary concern and that color was secondary: "A painting must possess maximum moral content; the design must be agreeable in itself and *the color should not provoke any sensorial attraction that will prejudice the unity of vision.*"

Those who defended color used *naturalism* as their main weapon. "Painting is the imitation of real life and Nature," the colorists said, "and color is the most convincing medium to imitate it." In principle this idea is based on the naturalism of the Venetians in general and of Titian in particular. But the "imitation of real life and Nature" is also present in Flemish painting, especially in Rubens's work. As this controversy continued, a series of paintings by Rubens, the *Life of Marie de' Medicis*, was found in Paris, which prompted the colorists to call themselves *Rubénistes*.

Although blood was never actually spilled, the debates, attacks, and justifications were so passionate that some historians consider the dispute "the most important artistic movement to take place in France at the end of the seventeenth century." Finally, Charles Lebrun, president of the Academy, resolved the controversy by stating that "The function of color is to satisfy the eyes, whereas drawing satisfies the mind." According to a contemporary French historian, Roger de Piles, a great admirer of Rubens who sided with the defenders of color and chiaroscuro, the debate between the Poussinistes and the Rubénistes was in reality the beginning of a controversy about the Academy's rules of teaching, which were somewhat hostile to the imagination and creativity that were essential for artistic discovery, and through which it intended to control the art of painting.

74

75

Figs. 74 and 75. Nicolas Poussin, *David's Triumph*, the Prado, Madrid; Rubens, *The Straw Hat*, the National Gallery, London. The *Poussinistes* and *Rubénistes* fought an historic debate, with one side defending Poussin's emphasis on drawing, and the other Rubens's use of color.

Light and black painting: Goya (1746–1828)

It is said that Francisco de Goya y Lucientes was at the same time the last friend of the old masters and the first of the modern ones. As the most versatile artist of his time, it is not easy to classify Goya under any particular style, theme, or determined tendency. During the same year he painted the frescoes of San Antonio de la Florida in Madrid, and produced etchings of the *Los Caprichos* series, in which he fiercely attacked corrupt social and ecclesiastical practices. In 1776 he began a series of more than sixty sketches for the Royal Tapestry Factory, in which a bright, luminous, cheerful palette predominates (fig. 76). Forty years later he created his famous *black paintings*, anticipating the twentieth-century movement of *Expressionism*.

He painted the ladies and gentlemen of high society—the Duke of Alba, the royal family of Charles IV, the actress "la tirana"—and the "majos" and "majas" of Madrid, fighting and falling under the bullets of French execution squads. In addition to his two famous paintings on the subject of Spain's war against Napoleon, *The Second of May* and *The Third of May 1808*, Goya made a series of etchings called *The Disasters of War*.

Goya never committed himself to a particular style, moving freely from one to another. His Spanish contemporaries debated the remnants of the Rococo and the majority followed the dictates of *Neoclassicism*; in France, Jacques-Louis David was recognized as the indisputable master of the latter style. Although throughout Europe pictures were being painted on the themes of ancient history, with their subjects dressed like Greeks and Romans, Goya continued to paint in his own special way, stating: "I have only three masters: Nature, Velázquez, and Rembrandt." By adding his own vision and personal style to their models he created such luminous works as *Lechera de Burdeos*, whose composition, color, and craft place the painting of the forefront of *Impressionism*.

Figs. 76 and 77. Francisco de Goya (1746–1828), *The Carriage Driver* and *The Lecture*. The Prado, Madrid.

76

77

Though the two paintings are somewhat contradictory in approach and craft, they are good examples of Goya's versatile and independent style. Goya avoided painting in the Rococo and Neoclassical styles, the fashionable styles of his day.

78

Pastel and watercolor (eighteenth century)

Watercolors were first used by the Egyptians about 3,000 years ago for painting on papyrus and parchment. Albrecht Dürer revived their use in the fifteenth century, and Leonardo da Vinci first used pastels around the same time. But neither media significantly influenced the art world until the eighteenth century, when watercolor was revived by English artists, including Sandby, Cozens, and De Wint, and pastels were used in portrait paintings by Quentin de La Tour, Carriera, Chardin, and Perroneau.

On this page an assortment of pastel colors is shown: 192 Grumbacher colors (fig. 78), 330 Rembrandt colors (fig. 79), and 528 Sennelier colors (fig. 81). We should remember that a wide selection is necessary because pastels are applied directly to a surface, making mixing difficult. We must also remember that Canson Mi-Teintes colored papers provide the best support for pastel colors. Chalks are in many ways very similar to pastels, although they have a rougher texture. They are available in several ranges of colors, such as the gray set at right (fig. 80).

As you may know, watercolors are available in either palette or tube form (figs. 82A and B): The choice is a matter of personal preference. A quality paper of no less than 250 grams—a rather thick sheet—is necessary. In addition to sable or synthetic brushes (figs. 83A and B), it is useful to have a sponge (fig. 83C) and absorbent paper (fig. 83D) for soaking up excess paint and for wringing out brushes. To reserve the whites of the paper you should use masking fluid (fig. 83E; always take care to apply it with a synthetic brush, never a sable one) and some cotton swabs (fig. 83F), or first sketch the areas with a white wax crayon (fig. 83G). Of course, watercolor "purists" do not accept the "sacrilege" of painting whites with gouache: The white must be the white of the paper.

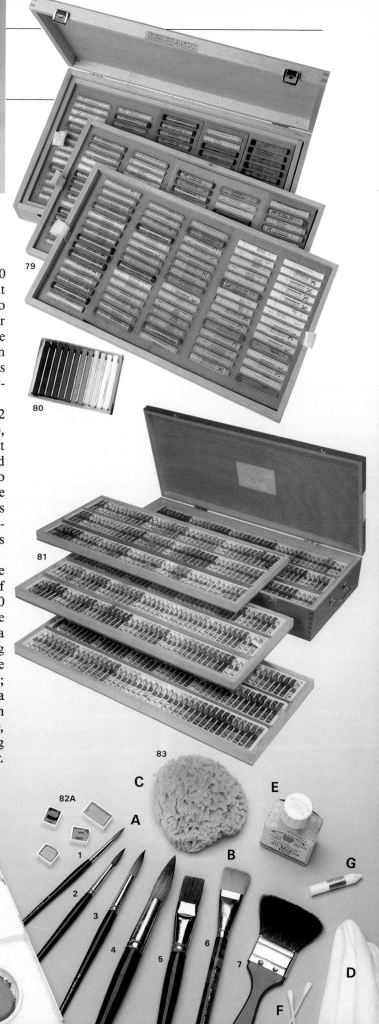

79

80

81

83

C

E

82A

A

1

B

G

2

3

4

5

6

7

82B

82A

D

F

The first abstractionist: Turner (1775–1851)

Joseph Mallord William Turner embarked on his remarkable artistic career at the age of fourteen by painting exclusively in watercolor. Though he began using oils in his early twenties, he continued to use both media throughout his life.

Turner was principally an enthusiastic follower of the *Romantic* movement, portraying passionate themes and the cosmic forces of nature—avalanches, earth, wind, and fire—in his first works in oil.

Turner's poetic representations of the phenomena of nature continued with his successive journeys to Italy and Venice. The color and light of the sky, the waters of the canals, and the buildings of Venice silhouetted through the mist and fog inspired him to paint his best watercolors, and later to convert forms into tints of color and light. As Turner hardly touched on figurative themes during the last years of his life, he became a forerunner of abstract art.

Turner died a recluse, living under a false name in a run-down house on the Thames. He was a strange man, an introvert, and an escapist, but he was a genius. He willed the body of his work—300 paintings and about 20,000 drawings and watercolors—to the government of England.

84

85

Ingres (1780–1867) versus Delacroix (1789–1863)

Ingres was a great master at the French Royal Academy, an uncompromising defender of exactitude and precision of line and form. Delacroix was a Romantic par excellence, both passionate and violent, without rules to encumber his creativity.

They were different; they thought in different ways. Ingres once said, "The drawing is everything, it is art in itself." Delacroix was of the opinion that "painters who are not colorists are illuminators, but they will never be painters." They hated each other. When Delacroix was approved

87

86

as a member of the Academy, Ingres exploded: "I find this brute to be such a stupid and ignorant painter that I want to break with the Academy!" For his part, Delacroix said of Ingres's work: "It is the total expression of an incomplete intelligence."

These two great masters were always at loggerheads with each other: Ingres, the more classical and perfect artist of drawing; Delacroix, the rebellious and revolutionary artist of color. But it is clear who won; we only have to look ahead thirty years to the exhibition at the home of photographer Paul Nadar, number 35 Boulevard des Capucines, Paris.

Figs. 84 and 85. (Opposite page) J. M. W. Turner (1775–1851), *Cottage Destroyed by an Avalanche* and *Light and Color.* The Tate Gallery, London. These examples of Turner's interpretation of the sublime and the extraordinary foreshadowed abstract art.

Fig. 86. Ingres (1780–1867), *The Spring.* The Louvre, Paris. Throughout his career Ingres embraced an academic exactness and rigidity which on occasion met with a cold interpretation: "It's all too

perfect," exclaimed the philosopher Ortega y Gasset. For this reason Ingres never acknowledged Delacroix's innovations.

Fig. 87. Eugène Delacroix (1789–1863), *Freedom Leading the People.* The Louvre, Paris. Delacroix was Ingres's opposite: a restless, perceptive romantic, and above all a colorist, he disliked Ingres's static style. Delacroix's open style inspired the Impressionists' early efforts.

"The first impression": Manet (1832–1883) and Monet (1840–1926)

Since the mid-eighteenth century, the Louvre in Paris has hosted an annual fine arts exhibition called the *Salon*, in which thousands of paintings and sculptures are displayed. In the past work was accepted or rejected by an often biased jury whose decisions were loudly criticized. In 1863 the jury rejected about 2,000 pictures and 1,000 sculptures, causing such a scandal that another salon was organized, the *Salon des Refusés*. That same year, Manet's *Luncheon on the Grass*, also accepted by the Salon, was the object of jokes and sarcastic comments by the more than 7,000 visitors. Paintings by Monet, Pissarro, Renoir, Cézanne, and Guillaumin were also exhibited. Two years later, at the Salon of 1865, the display of Manet's painting *Olympia* (fig. 88) unleashed a howl of public protest and criticism. Théophile Gautier wrote in *Le Moniteur*: "*Olympia* is nothing more than a sickly woman lying on a meat-colored sheet; the modeling is worthless . . ." Finally, Manet, Pissarro, Renoir, Cézanne, and Sisley, among others, decided to organize their own exhibition, which took place on 15 April 1874, in the rooms of the photographer Paul Nadar, at number 35 Boulevard des Capucines. Among the many paintings exhibited was one by Monet called *Impression, Sunrise*, which was criticized by Louis Leroy, who imagined how an artist would react to Monet's work: "Impression . . . so I'm impressed, there must be some kind of impression here." From this ironic statement the term *Impressionists* was coined, referring to the group of painters who until then had been known as "Manet's gang." Although the exhibition was a critical failure, Manet and Monet continued to work in and defend their techniques of painting, along with such artists as Pissarro, Cézanne, Degas, Renoir, Berthe Morisot, Sisley, Guillaumin, and Whistler. Later,

Impressionism gained universal recognition as the movement that shifted the emphasis in painting from historical, religious, or mythical subjects in large formats rendered in dark colors and produced in the studio, to everyday motifs, with a focus on color and light, painted directly from nature.

Figs. 88 and 89. Édouard Manet (1832–1883), *Olympia*, the Louvre, Paris; *The People of Berne Street*, private collection. Although Manet began the movement that was to be called "Impressionism" with his paintings *The Fife Player*, *Luncheon on the Grass*, and *Olympia*, he did not take part in any of the eight exhibitions organized by Degas and resented the movement's first nickname, "Manet's Gang."

88

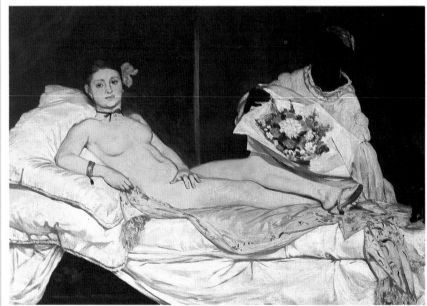

89

91

Figs. 90 to 92. Claude Monet (1840–1926), *Snow in Vétheuil* and *Saint-Lazare Station*, the Louvre, Paris; *Woman with a Parasol and Child*, the National Gallery, London. Monet took part in all of the Impressionists' exhibitions and was probably the most representative, as much for his outdoor paintings as for his interest in investigating the effects of light and color on form. A good example of this can be seen in his paintings of the cathedral at Reims; the *Water Lilies* series, painted in his garden at Giverny, of which he drew many sketches; and several paintings and *paneaus*, on display in the two large salons at L'Orangerie, Paris.

90

92

Chevreul (1786–1889), dyer of Gobelins

In 1824, professor of chemistry Michel-Eugène Chevreul was named director of dyeworks at the Gobelins Tapestry Works, founded by Henry IV of France in 1601. In addition to making important discoveries and supervising research, Chevreul wrote a book in 1839 entitled *The Law of Simultaneous Contrast and Harmonization of Colors*, establishing the scientific principles of Impressionist and Neoimpressionist painting. (These concepts will be discussed later on in this book.) In another of his books, *Colors and Their Applications to the Industrial Arts* (1864), Chevreul compiled and illustrated with color wheels 14,400 colors used since antiquity, attempting to examine, classify, name, and determine the characteristics of every color that has ever existed. This may seem to be a somewhat exaggerated number, but not if we consider that by the end of the eighteenth century a count was carried out—more or less scientifically—resulting in a total of 30,000 different colors.

The graph in figure 93 is a summary of Chevreul's findings. From left to right we can see when and in what order colors came into use: Humans had only six colors in the prehistoric period; by 3000 B.C. the Egyptians had added five more. From there we continue from ancient Greece and Rome, up through the twentieth century.

Fig. 93. The graph below shows the evolution of color pigments from prehistory to the present day. For example, *Egyptian blue* was developed 3000 B.C., *ultramarine blue* around the seventh century A.D., and *Prussian blue* in the nineteenth century.

THE EVOLUTION OF COLOR PIGMENTS

93

30000 B.C.	3000 B.C.	2000 B.C.	1000 B.C.	1st Century

Oil colors

Oil paints today are made in practically the same way as in van Eyck's day, with powdered color or *pigment* mixed into a liquid *binder*. What has changed, however, is the way in which they are made and stored. For hundreds of years, painters made their own paints in the studio. In the mid-nineteenth century, manufacturers began producing high-quality oils. Oil paints were generally kept in small bags of animal hide, which the artist would puncture with a nail to squeeze out the color. This rather primitive practice continued until 1840, when Winsor & Newton invented a glass file in the shape of a syringe. One year later, the now widespread metal tube was developed.

As you may already know, the most common support for oil painting is canvas or cotton mounted on a wooden stretcher; but it is also possible to paint with oils on cardboard, wood, and paper. Brushes are normally made of hog's hair, but it is better to use sable or squirrel hair brushes for resolving forms. Most painters use either linseed oil or turpentine as a solvent, or a mixture of the two in equal parts. It is also necessary to have a spatula handy for scraping and correcting or for cleaning the palette. Last, the painter must have some rags and old newspapers, which are indispensable for cleaning brushes.

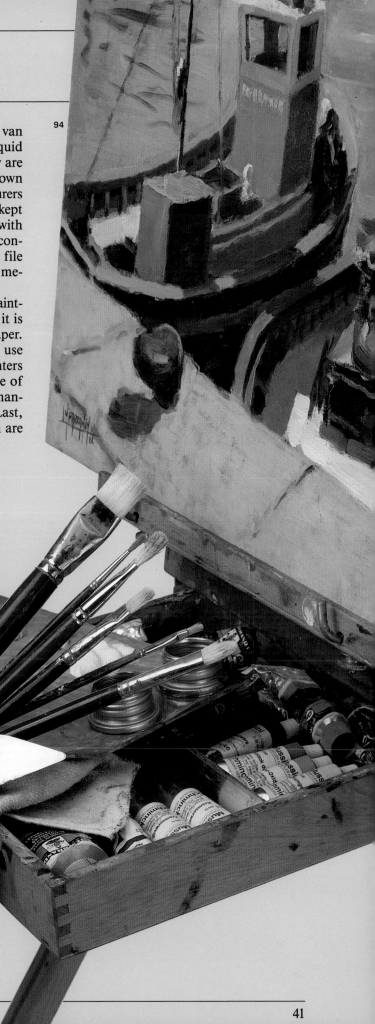

Century   20th Century

PLASTER WHITE
LEAD WHITE
ZINC WHITE
TITIAN WHITE
GRAY
NAPLES YELLOW
CADMIUM YELLOW
ROYAL YELLOW
YELLOW OCHER
SIENNA
SEPIA
BITUMEN
SINOPIA RED
RED
VERMILION
CADMIUM RED
RED LAKE
ALIZARIN
TYRIAN PURPLE
MALACHITE GREEN
VERDIGRIS
EARTH GREEN
EMERALD GREEN
CERULEAN BLUE
COBALT BLUE
EGYPTIAN BLUE
ULTRAMARINE BLUE
PRUSSIAN BLUE
PHTHALO BLUE
DARK VIOLET
SMOKE BLACK
IVORY BLACK

Seurat's optical mixing (1859–1891)

Georges Seurat was a great enthusiast of science and aesthetics, and an avid student of theories of color and vision. His many publications and investigative work on the absorption and reflection of colors brought him to the conclusion that the effects of *additive synthesis*, or the merging of colors by the eye, could be reproduced in a painting through *optical mixing*, thus substituting the mixture of the palette for the combination of reflected light of small colored dots on the retina. To explain it more clearly, we should say, for example, that to depict green Seurat applied tiny yellow and blue dots, each one directly next to the other, which seen from a distance look green. Seurat's first major painting, considered to be the most successful example of this technique, which he called *Divisionism*, was his *Sunday on the Island of La Grande Jatte* (fig. 97). Art historians have also referred to this technique as *Chromoluminarism, Neoimpressionism*, and *Pointillism*, the latter being the most widely used term.

Pointillism was practiced by Signac, Dubois-Pillet, Cross, Luce, and many others. Pisarro painted some Pointillist pictures, then returned to Impressionism. Van Gogh and Gauguin also experimented briefly with Pointillism.

Figs. 95 and 96. Additive synthesis: The boxed portion of the image, enlarged in figure 96, demonstrates that the breakdown of color into dots (cyan, magenta, yellow, and black) produces the appropriate colors when combined.

Fig. 97. Georges Seurat (1859–1891), *Sunday on the Island of La Grande Jatte*. The Art Institute of Chicago.

95

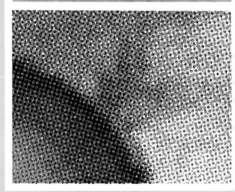

A

96

97

Cézanne (1839–1906), the forerunner of modern painting

Renoir described Cézanne as "beastly and terrible, like disturbed divinity." Renoir explained that sometimes when Cézanne was painting he would suddenly shout "I'll never finish! Never! Never!" On other occasions, after a hard day's work he would take up his spatula and scrape off everything he had done... or simply throw the picture out of the window. Was he a perfectionist? Yes, but not when it came to "touching up" the picture, only when it came to finding and capturing "sensations" that he felt when in front of the model. For that reason he was a slow painter; for that reason he would shout, "I'll never finish!" For that very same reason Cézanne dissociated himself from the Impressionists; according to him, they were only trying to capture an impression, and he wanted—in his own words—"to transform that impression into something solid and lasting." Of course, he was the forerunner of modern painting.

Cézanne was the only painter who did not allow himself to become absorbed in the model; instead, he painted what *he* wanted, thanks to his tremendous effort to become closer to nature, which meant freeing himself from the bondage of painting an identical copy of the subject.

In August 1906, a month and a half before his death at the age of seventy-seven, Cézanne wrote in a letter to his friend and fellow painter Emile Bernard: "I continue to study the nature that surrounds me and I believe I am progressing somewhat. I would like to have you here with me because I feel very lonely. I am old and sick. I have sworn to die painting."

Fig. 98. Paul Cézanne (1839–1906), *The Blue Vase*. The Louvre, Paris.

Fig. 99. Cézanne, *Sainte-Victoire Mountain*. Musée d'Orsay, Paris.

Fig. 100. Cézanne, *Bathers*. Pushkin Museum, Moscow.

99

98

100

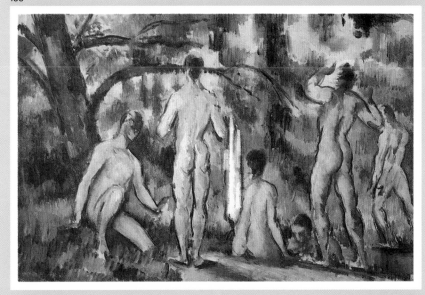

Van Gogh (1853–1890), the madman

101

On the afternoon of 27 July 1890, in a wheat field in Auvers-Sur-Oise, Vincent van Gogh shot himself in the chest. He died two days later with his brother Theo at his side. Among the mourners at his funeral were Père Tanguy, Emile Bernard, and Lucien Pisarro. There was no mention of his death in the obituary columns. It was only the death of a poor, mad artist. On 29 July 1990 an extraordinary exhibition of 133 of van Gogh's paintings ended, marking the centenary of his death. The exhibition was sponsored by Her Majesty Queen of the Netherlands, and twenty-five dignitaries—ambassadors, prime ministers, ministers, and cultural attachés—served on the board of directors. The paintings were loaned from forty-eight museums in various countries as well as from dozens of private collections, and the exhibition was visited by more than 1.5 million people, with lines stretching up to 4 miles long.

Van Gogh sold only one painting during his life: *Red Vineyards in Arles*, for 400 francs. In 1990 at Sotheby's auction house in New York, the madman's painting sold for $53.9 million.

Fig. 101. Vincent van Gogh (1853–1890), *Garden in Arles*. Private collection.

Fig. 102. *The Roulin Postman*. Museum of Fine Arts, Boston.

Fig. 103. *Armand Roulin*. Folkwang, Essen, Switzerland.

Fig. 104. *Starry Night*. The Museum of Modern Art, New York.

Fig. 105. *The Sand at Arles*. The Hermitage, Saint Petersburg.

Fig. 106. *Room in Arles*. Rijksmuseum, Amsterdam.

102

103

104

105

106

The Fauves (1905)

In the main exhibition hall of the 1905 Autumn Salon, a series of paintings were put on display that broke tradition with everything that had been done before—simplified and distorted drawings with pure, flat, and violent colors, red faces with green shadows, a street of green cobblestones—pictures that everyone found absurd.

Though some of these artists, such as Matisse and Albert Marquet, were relatively well-known, most were obscure, having exhibited only once or twice. Also on display in the main hall were a sculpture of a child's torso and a bust of a woman by Marquet, whose forms were similar to those used in fifteenth-century Florence. When Louis Vauxcelles, a critic for the avant-garde magazine *Gil Blas*, entered the hall on the opening day of the exhibit, he exclaimed—looking directly at Matisse—*"Donatello chez les fauves!"* (Donatello in the beasts' house!) His utterance was published in that magazine and, exactly as had happened with the Impressionists, the name *Fauves* stuck with this distinctive group of painters, which included Derain, Vlaminck, Rouault, Manguin, Camoin, Jean Puy, and Othon Friesz.

107

108

109

The Fauves became the first modernists to justify Maurice Denis's advice, in what has become one of the most celebrated war cries in the history of modern art:

Remember that before a painting is a horse, a nude, or any other motif, it is essentially a flat surface that is covered with colors in a certain order.

Fig. 107. (Opposite page) Alexej Jawlensky (1864–1941), *Still-life with White Horse*. Private collection, Lugano.

Fig. 108. Maurice de Vlaminck (1876–1958), *Portrait of Derain*. Private collection.

Fig. 109. André Derain (1880–1954), *The Happy One*. National Museum of Modern Art, Pompidou Center, Paris.

Fig. 110. Derain, *Portrait of Matisse*. The Tate Gallery, London.

Fig. 111. Derain, *The Bridge at Westminster*. Private collection, Paris.

Fig. 112. Derain, *The Colliure Bridge*. Museum of Modern Art; gift of Pierre and Denis Levy.

Picasso's "periods" (1881–1973), Cubism, and the "isms"

In 1901, at the age of twenty-eight, having painted in charcoal and pastels in a style similar to Toulouse Lautrec's and reminiscent of *Pointillism* and *Fauvism*, Pablo Picasso began his celebrated *Blue Period*. For the next four years, his only subjects were "the poor, beggars, the sick, the disabled, the hungry, and prostitutes." Some biographers attribute this period of depression to the suicide of Picasso's close friend Casajemas, but it was also due to the extreme cold of those winters and the many privations that Picasso suffered while he lived for four years in Paris and Barcelona.

In 1905, the artist made an effort, in the words of his biographer Martini, "to calm his emotive violence and search for a serene and joyful tonic

in the form of circus artists, such as acrobats, tightrope walkers, horse-riders, and the like." This radical change became known as his *Pink Period*, in which he abandoned his use of predominately *cool* colors and began to paint only with colors of the *warm* range. It was not a sudden transition from the dominant blue tones shown in fig. 113; Picasso worked through the gray range to gradually introduce pink (fig. 114), ending up with pink figures on red backgrounds.

By the winter of 1906 Picasso was a famous artist. He had painted more than two hundred pictures, and had started to sculpt in wood and produce excellent etchings. Thanks to the patronage of the Stein brothers and the Russian merchant Scukin,

who were keen buyers, he could continue in the same style, as an Impressionist, or choose to work as a Fauvist. But Picasso was looking for something new; he was concerned with structure and the spatial representation of form. Against his friends' advice he began to work on a type of painting that broke all the rules—of perspective, modeling, light,

Fig. 113. Pablo Picasso (1881–1973), *Life.* Cleveland Museum of Art; gift of The Hanna Foundation. After many preliminary sketches and paintings, this is Picasso's final version of *Life.*

Fig. 114. Picasso, *Harlequin on a Horse.* Collection of Mr. and Mrs. Mellon, United States. This image was painted by Picasso in 1905, at the beginning of his Pink Period.

113

114

and shadow—in Western art. After working feverishly on more than twenty sketches and drawings, in the spring of 1907 he painted the first *Cubist* painting, *Les Demoiselles d'Avignon*. One of the most famous paintings of contemporary art, it transformed the expectations and theories of art for all time.

In effect, Picasso went from Cubism, which favored form over color, to the *geometric abstraction* or *collage Cubism* of 1913, which demanded that form dominate the image completely. *Expressionism*, where color was again the protagonist, followed later, with a series of other *isms: Futurism, Op Art* and *Pop Art, Hyperrealism*, and so on, in which color is omnipresent and in certain cases is a decisive element of the picture.

Fig. 115. Andy Warhol (1930–1987), *Marilyn*. Leder Gallery. Warhol created a series of famous portraits that he executed with a special technique: printing the same image several times while changing the color range and introducing special effects with the contrast of juxtaposed colors, such as with this print of Marilyn Monroe, one of the most popular and identifiable pieces of Pop Art.

Fig. 116. Wassily Kandinsky (1866–1944), *Yellow, Red, and Blue*. Museum of Modern Art, Pompidou Center, Paris.

Fig. 117. Robert Delaunay (1889–1941), *Solar Discs*. The Museum of Modern Art, New York.

115

116

117

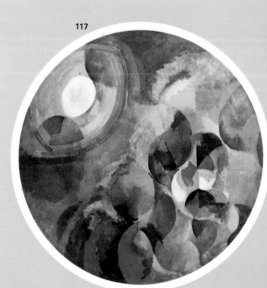

Isaac Newton discovered that color is light. Thomas Young used three colors to recreate all the colors of the spectrum. James Clerk Maxwell and Heinrich Hertz established that light travels in waves. Hermann von Helmholtz and Thomas Young discovered the physiological mechanisms that regulate color vision. Michel-Eugène Chevreul formulated the laws of simultaneous contrast and color harmony.... In this section examine what these scientists did that enable us to paint better pictures; this knowledge "is not superfluous" as Delacroix stated, but rather constitutes the principles that all artists should know, for it is untrue to say that "you can learn to draw but you must be born to paint."

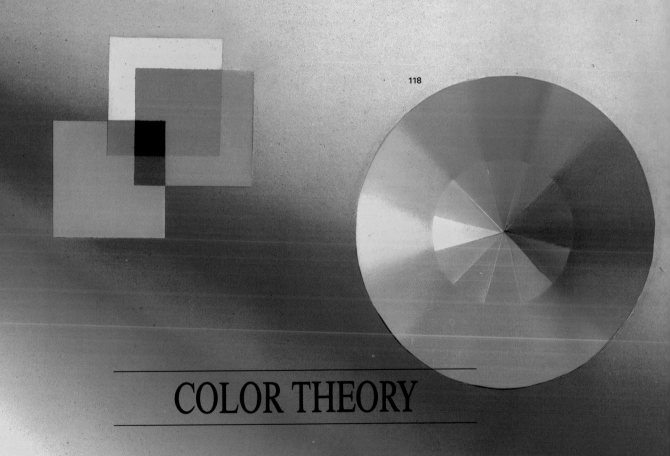

COLOR THEORY

Newton and Young

Just over three hundred years ago, a young student at Trinity College, Cambridge, revealed one of the most important discoveries of natural science: the *law of gravitation*. Isaac Newton—for this was his name—became so famous for this discovery that his contemporaries attached no importance to some of his other inventions, which include calculus and the theory of light and color. Newton described the latter in his diary: "I have a triangular glass prism to carry out experiments on the well-known phenomena of colors. After pulling down the blind and making a hole in it to let in the right amount of sunlight, I placed my prism at the opening to refract the light onto the opposite wall. It was most pleasing to contemplate the intensely bright colors thus obtained." Those "intensely bright colors" were, in fact, white light refracted into the colors of the spectrum: a fundamental step toward the under-standing that *color is light* (fig. 120). These are the colors of the spectrum:

Dark blue
Light blue
Green
Yellow
Red
Purple

During a sun shower, each raindrop acts like Newton's prism, and these millions of prisms produce a rainbow (figs. 121 and 122).
According to Newton, color is light; as we see the colors of objects as they receive light, Newton's discovery leads us to conclude that the spectrum contains all the colors of nature.
One hundred years later in London, a scientist and physician named Thomas Young made a thorough study of color theory.
Based on Newton's discovery, Young carried out the following experiment. Each of six lamps was fitted with a lens of one of the six colors of the spectrum. Young then lit the lamps and, by changing and omitting light rays, he made a new and definitive finding:

Fig. 119. In addition to the theory of gravitation and calculus, Isaac Newton also discovered the nature of light; that is, that light is color.

Fig. 120. If you project a beam of light through a small hole and hold a prism in its path, the light will be refracted into the colors of the spectrum.

Figs. 121 and 122. A rainbow is formed by rays of sunlight passing through raindrops, which act as prisms.

The six colors of the spectrum could be reduced to the three primary colors (red, green, and dark blue), which could then be added together again to produce white light.

This helps us to understand what an additive primary color is: All the colors of the spectrum can be reduced to and composed of three basic colors—red, green, and dark blue.

I have carried out a similar experiment with three lamps, and can vouch for the authenticity of the original (fig. 123). During his experiment, Young reached another important conclusion. By superimposing the lights of the three lamps in pairs, a second set of three lighter colors could be obtained: *yellow*, by adding red and green; *purple*, by adding red and dark blue; and *light blue*, by adding green and dark blue. These are called secondary colors.

Until now, we have discussed beams of light, and breaking down and reconstructing white light. We are talking about *light* colors, which fall into the following two categories:

PRIMARY LIGHT COLORS
Dark blue
Green
Red

SECONDARY LIGHT COLORS
Yellow
Purple
Light blue

Of course, these are not an *artist's* colors—we paint with *pigment* colors, not *light* colors. But we will discuss this point later.

Fig. 123. Thomas Young used the lamp experiment to show that with only three colors—red, green, and blue—it was possible to reconstruct white light.

123

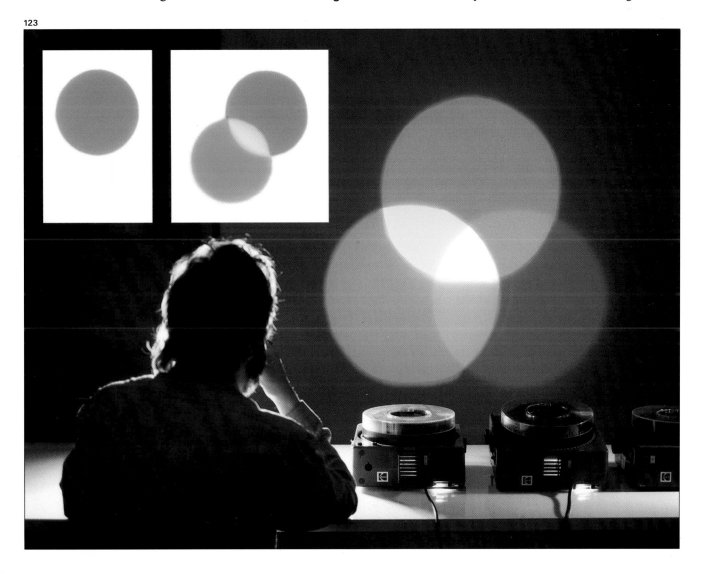

Color names

As you know, the spectrum is made up of six colors. Certain books refer to a seven-color spectrum, but there are actually only six. This fact has been scientifically demonstrated, first by *photomechanical color selection* (used by the graphic arts industry), then by *inverted color films*—color transparencies or slides—which were invented by Agfa and Kodak in 1936. These films use the *tripack system*, which is made up of three light-sensitive emulsions: one sensitive to yellow, another to red, and the third to blue. In 1936 Agfa and Kodak also introduced two new color names that were later adopted by the graphic arts industry for color printing.

Purple is called
MAGENTA

Light blue is called
CYAN BLUE

In the 1950s, the DIN Standards of color identification, numbers 16.508 and 15.509, adopted these names to define basic printing colors. Until the late 1980s, no color chart referred to *magenta* or *cyan blue*. Today, all color manufacturers have included or are in the process of including *magenta* and *cyan blue*.

My own proposal confirms *cyan blue* and *magenta*, changing *dark blue* to *blue* or *violet-blue* and accepting the remaining names, *green, yellow,* and *red*. Remember that these will be the color names used in this book to refer to the colors of the spectrum.

Fig. 124. Most people talk of seven or more colors when referring to the spectrum: It is usual for people to include *orange* and *lilac* or *indigo*, and not to know what kind of blue *"cyan blue"* is. The author of *Color*, Harald Küppers, states that scientists usually use the names listed in the third column. While basically accepting the previous names, I propose the names shown in the fourth column.

124

MOST COMMON COLOR NAMES	COLOR NAMES PROPOSED BY KÜPPERS	COLOR NAMES USED BY SCIENTISTS	COLOR NAMES USED IN THIS BOOK	COLORS OF THE SPECTRUM
LILAC				
VIOLET	VIOLET	BLUE	BLUE	
BLUE	CYAN BLUE	CYAN BLUE	CYAN BLUE	
GREEN	GREEN	GREEN	GREEN	
YELLOW	YELLOW	YELLOW	YELLOW	
ORANGE				
RED	ORANGE	RED	RED	
PURPLE	MAGENTA	MAGENTA	MAGENTA	

Maxwell and Hertz: electromagnetic waves

In 1873 James Clerk Maxwell, a Scottish physicist and a pupil of the English scientist Michael Farady, published a series of equations concerning the electromagnetic theory of light showing that light is the result of the simultaneous spread of an electric field and a magnetic field. At the same time, the German physicist Heinrich Hertz, who knew of Maxwell and his calculations, managed to produce electromagnetic waves using an oscillator, demonstrating that they had all the properties of light rays—reflection and refraction, interference, diffraction, and polarization—and that they traveled at a speed of 300,000 kilometers a second. In order to understand what electromagnetic waves are, we must first remember that light rays are energy and form only a small part of the entire energy spectrum. The lengths of the various kinds of waves range from a millionth of a millimeter up to several thousand kilometers. For easier calculating, short wavelengths are measured in *nanometers* (nm), which are thousand millionths of a meter.

The figure below (fig. 125) shows the scale of electromagnetic waves in this unit of measurement. Light oscillates between 380 and 720 nm (A), with ultraviolet rays, x-rays (B), gamma and alpha rays (C) with wave radiation of a thousand millionth of a meter. On the right are the electromagnetic wavelengths that produce heat (D), television (E), radio (F), and electricity (G); the latter has wavelengths of 1,000 kilometers.

Fig. 125. Basing his work on the research carried out by the Scottish physicist James Clerk Maxwell, the German physicist Heinrich Hertz discovered that light is composed of electromagnetic waves of various lengths, measured in *nanometers* (nm). Below is a scale of electromagnetic waves showing light oscillating between 380 and 720 nm.

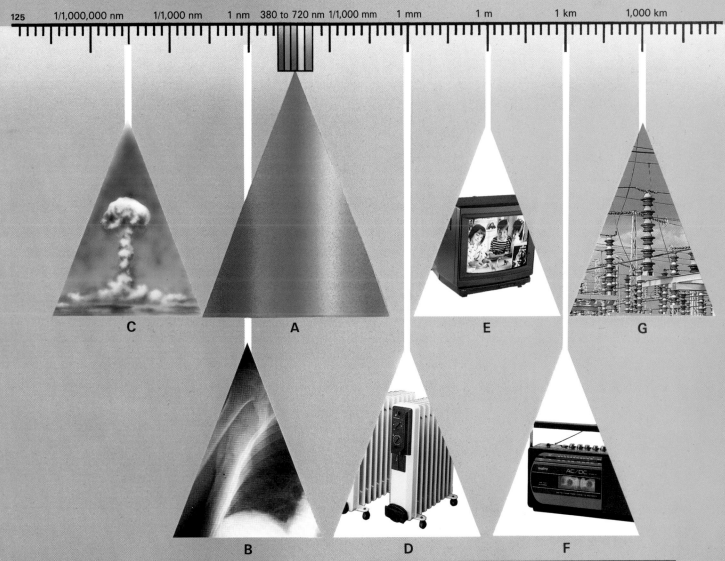

125 1/1,000,000 nm   1/1,000 nm   1 nm   380 to 720 nm   1/1,000 mm   1 mm   1 m   1 km   1,000 km

C   A   E   G

B   D   F

Absorption and reflection

Why are tomatoes red? Why are lemons yellow? Why are the leaves on a tree green?

To answer these questions we must bear in mind:

- *First, that color is light.*
- *Second, that six colors make up white light.*
- *And third, that these six colors can be reduced to three: red, green, and blue.*

The answer is that *all objects are made up of substances that absorb and reflect colors*; in other words, *they absorb and reflect electromagnetic waves.* So when a white object receives the three primary *light colors* (red, green, and blue), it *reflects* them all and together they create white (fig. 126A). If the object is black (B), the opposite occurs: it *absorbs* the three *light colors*, leaving the object without light, so it looks black to us.

The same thing happens in a darkened room: Although it contains a blue carpet, a red armchair, and so on, we see neither the carpet nor the armchair because the dark negates light and color. Now watch what happens with the red object or cube (C) in figure 126; it receives the three *light colors*, absorbing green and blue and reflecting red. Notice also that the yellow cube (D) absorbs blue and reflects red and green that when combined, as you remember, produce yellow. The three *light colors* also hit the magenta-colored cube (E), but it absorbs green and reflects red and blue, which together produce magenta.

This phenomena of absorption and reflection shows us how light creates the colors of objects by *adding together* electromagnetic waves. We will analyze this point later. Now we will discuss how color is perceived through vision.

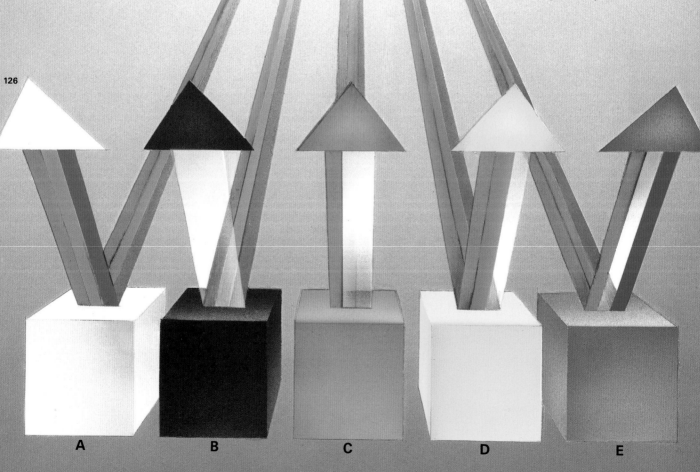

Fig. 126. The color of objects is based on the phenomenon of absorption and reflection of light, or rather the light colors of the spectrum reduced to three: red, green, and blue. So while a white object (A) absorbs and reflects all the colors, a yellow object (D) receives the three light colors, absorbing the blue and reflecting the red and the green, which together produce yellow.

126

A   B   C   D   E

How we see color

Thanks to the eye, one of the most marvelous organs of the human body, we are able to see color. Similar to a camera, the eye has a *cornea*, which acts as a protective lens; an *iris* and a *pupil*, which serve as an aperture; and a *crystalline lens*, which acts as a zoom. The *retina* is the "instant film" connected to the *brain* by the *optic nerve*, where the images and colors are reproduced (fig. 127). Leaving aside the analogy with the camera, let's focus on the structure and the functions of the retina (fig. 128), a membrane so fine that although it measures less than half a millimeter thick it has a fabulous microscopic capacity, as it contains 120 million *rods* and 6 million *cones*. The *cones* and *rods* are *photorecep-*

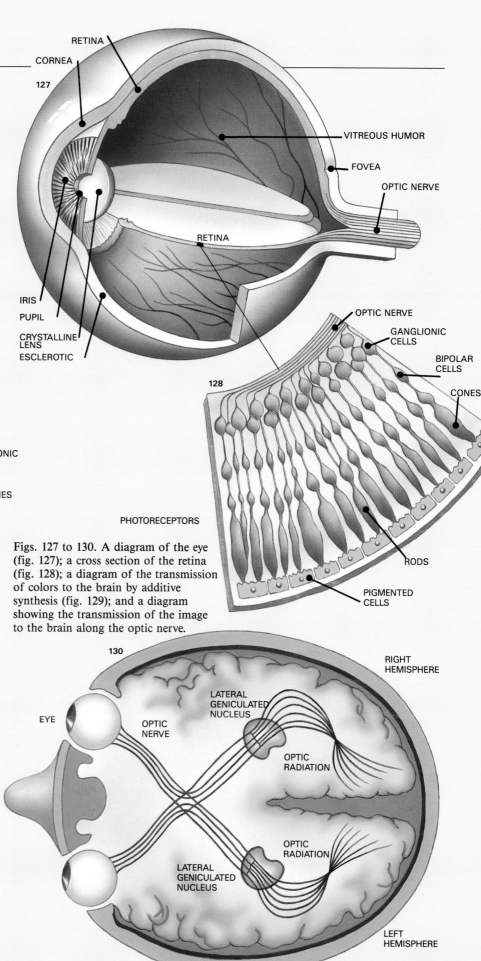

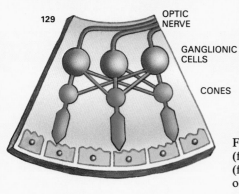

PHOTORECEPTORS

Figs. 127 to 130. A diagram of the eye (fig. 127); a cross section of the retina (fig. 128); a diagram of the transmission of colors to the brain by additive synthesis (fig. 129); and a diagram showing the transmission of the image to the brain along the optic nerve.

tors, which are sensory cells that capture and encode the different wavelengths of light. This radiation, which is translated into the light colors *blue, green,* and *red*, reproduces images by means of *additive synthesis* (fig. 129), a system comparable to that used in television, which we will discuss later. The images, transformed into electrical impulses, are sent to the *optic nerve* through the bipolar and ganglionic cells.

Finally, the *optic nerve* communicates the retina's information to the brain, which then develops this visual information, analyzing the details of shape, color, depth, and movement (fig. 130).

LIGHT colors: additive synthesis

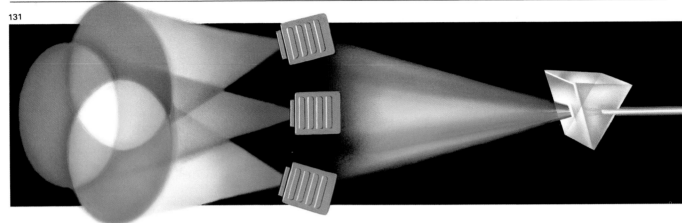

131

As we said earlier, Isaac Newton broke light down into the colors of the spectrum by placing a triangular glass prism in the path of a ray of light. Based on this experiment, he reached the conclusion that *light is color*. To confirm his discovery, Newton then placed a second prism in the path of the spectrum, which recomposed it and projected a point of white light on the wall. Not satisfied with this experiment, Newton painted the colors of the spectrum on a wheel, placed it on a shaft, and spun it at a great speed. The colors first blended together, then the wheel turned white.

This experiment, known as *Newton's wheel*, is something you can easily do yourself, with a piece of cardboard, some form of color or pigment, and a drill with a sanding wheel. If you have a sanding wheel, all you need to do is cut the cardboard into a circle and paint the colors of spectrum on it (fig. 132); then stick or fasten this circle to the wheel on the drill and turn it on. When the circle begins to spin, the colors blend together but are still distinguishable (fig. 133). When the wheel is spun at full speed, the colors disappear and the circle turns completely white (fig. 134). This experiment and the reconstruction of light performed by Newton with two prisms (which was corroborated by Young when he superimposed the three beams of light; fig. 131), lead us to the conclusion that

Light "paints" by
ADDING COLORS.

To "paint" an object *white*, light adds together all of the *light* colors of the spectrum; to paint an object *yellow*, the light is composed of the light colors red and green. I must admit that when I carried out the experiment with the three lamps and saw that by mixing red and green I obtained yellow, I was astonished.

Fig. 131. Primary light colors mixed in pairs: red, blue, and green, by a process of *additive synthesis*, or *adding light colors*, to produce the secondary light colors: magenta, cyan blue, and yellow. The sum or mixture of the three primary light colors reconstructs white light.

Figs. 132 to 134. This duplicates the experiment carried out by Newton with his *color wheel*, which, when spinning at full speed, combines the colors by additive synthesis to reconstruct white "light." You can repeat this experiment with a color wheel (fig. 132) attached to the sanding wheel of a drill.

132

133

134

PIGMENT colors: subtractive synthesis

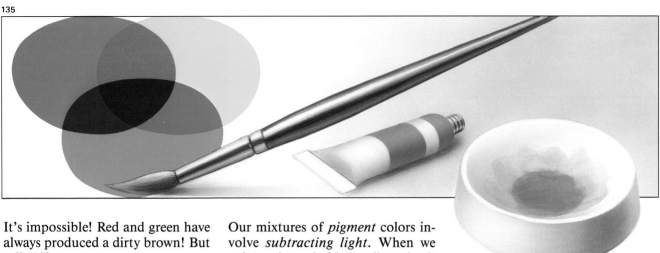

135

It's impossible! Red and green have always produced a dirty brown! But yellow!?

Fortunately, I soon realized that the yellow was a result of *adding together two light colors*; of course, by doubling the amount of light, a brighter light is obtained: the *light* color yellow (fig. 136).

In physics, obtaining color by adding together *light* colors is known as *additive synthesis*. Incidentally, we are able to view television thanks to the additive superimposing of the three *light* colors (red, green, and blue) distributed in 625 lines, which reproduce color images on the screen.

But we do not paint with light, we paint with pigments:

We cannot obtain *light* colors by mixing *pigment* colors.

Our mixtures of *pigment* colors involve *subtracting light*. When we paint a piece of white cardboard red, we are subtracting the *light* colors of green and blue from the white. To paint green, we mix yellow and cyan blue: the yellow absorbs (subtracts) the blue, and the cyan blue absorbs (subtracts) the red; the only color that is reflected is green (fig. 137). In

Fig. 135. *Pigment* colors behave differently than *light* colors: When the primary pigment colors (magenta, yellow, and cyan blue) are mixed in pairs, the process of *subtractive synthesis*, or *subtracting light*, will produce the darker, secondary pigment colors: red, blue, and green. The mixture of the three primary pigment colors produces black.

Fig. 136. ADDITIVE SYNTHESIS: In order to "paint" the secondary light color yellow, the *light* colors of red and green are mixed to create a lighter color, yellow.

Fig. 137. SUBTRACTIVE SYNTHESIS: In order to obtain the secondary pigment color green we mix blue and yellow. In light colors, cyan blue absorbs red light while yellow absorbs blue light. The only color that is reflected is green, obtained by subtracting blue and red.

physics this is called *subtractive synthesis*.

This is why our *primary pigment colors* must be lighter than the *primary light colors*. Based on the six colors of the spectrum, we may change the value or dominance of certain colors in relation to others, remembering that:

Our primary colors are the secondary LIGHT colors, and vice versa; our secondary colors are the primary LIGHT colors.

136

137

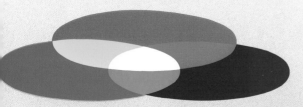

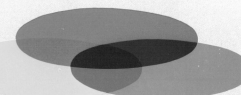

An artist's colors

Here are our *pigment* colors, classified into *primary, secondary, and ertiary*:

PRIMARY PIGMENT COLORS
(fig. 140)

Magenta
Yellow
Cyan blue

Mixing these primary pigment colors in pairs produces the following

SECONDARY PIGMENT COLORS
(fig. 140)

Magenta + Yellow = Red
Cyan blue + Yellow = Green
Cyan blue + Magenta = Blue

You can see these mixtures in figure 141 on the following page. Notice also that mixing our three primary colors gives black (fig. 140), which confirms that our colors *subtract* light and act by means of *subtractive synthesis*.

Now study the color wheel in figure 138, which is made up of our *pigment* colors. The three *primary* (P) colors appear, which, when mixed in pairs, produce the three *secondary* (S) colors, the secondary colors mixed with the primaries produce six more colors, which are called *tertiary* colors (T).

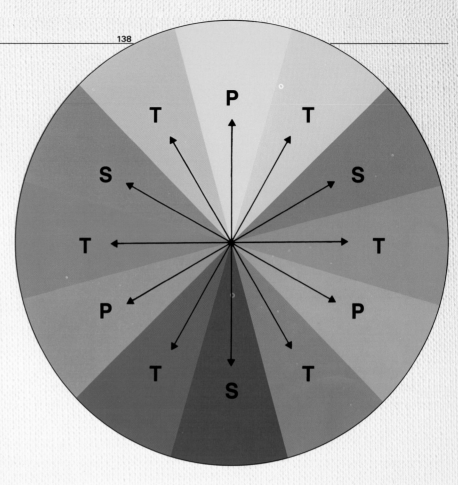

Figure 142 shows the six tertiary colors: emerald green, violet, ultramarine blue, crimson, light green, and orange.

Fig. 138. A color wheel painted with pigment colors made up of the primary colors (P), which when mixed in pairs produce the secondary colors (S), which in turn when mixed in pairs with the primaries produce the tertiary colors (T).

140

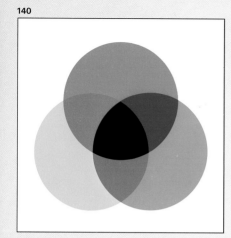

Figs. 139 and 143. In order to imitate the primary colors when painting in oil or watercolors you can use (from left to right) Prussian blue (as cyan blue), madder (as magenta), and lemon yellow (as yellow); and to imitate the secondary colors (fig. 139B), cadmium red (as red), emerald green (as green), and ultramarine blue (as blue).

Fig. 140. SUBTRACTIVE SYNTHESIS: Primary and secondary pigment colors that, when mixed together, subtract light and produce black.

Figs. 144 to 146. You must paint with the colors listed in figures 139 and 143 in order to imitate the primary colors, with colored pencils, pastels, or crayons.

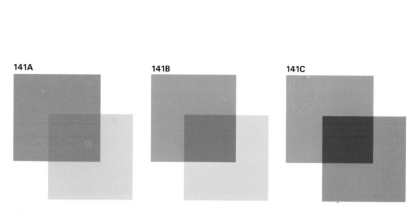

141A   141B   141C

Figs. 141 A, B, and C. Primary pigment colors mixed in pairs to obtain the secondary colors:

| Magenta + Yellow = Red | Cyan blue + Yellow = Green | Cyan blue + Magenta = Blue or dark blue |

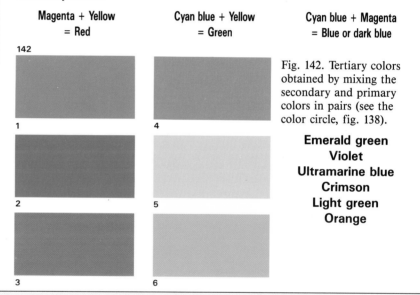

142

1   4

2   5

3   6

Fig. 142. Tertiary colors obtained by mixing the secondary and primary colors in pairs (see the color circle, fig. 138).

**Emerald green
Violet
Ultramarine blue
Crimson
Light green
Orange**

143   144   145   146

All the colors using only three colors

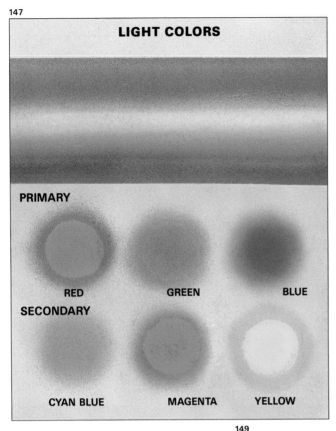

147

LIGHT COLORS

PRIMARY

RED   GREEN   BLUE

SECONDARY

CYAN BLUE   MAGENTA   YELLOW

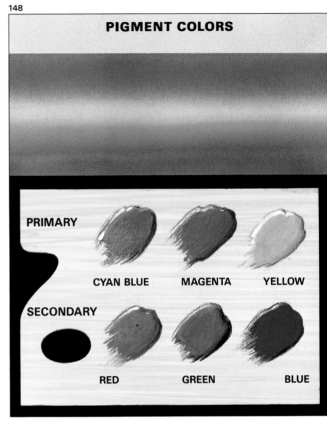

148

PIGMENT COLORS

PRIMARY

CYAN BLUE   MAGENTA   YELLOW

SECONDARY

RED   GREEN   BLUE

The two pictures at the top of the page remind us that the *light* colors that make up the spectrum are exactly the same *pigment* colors that we have on our palette. As you already know, the only difference between them is that the order of the *primary and secondary colors* is not the same: The *secondary light* colors are the *primary pigment* colors, and vice versa (figs. 147 and 148). But this is not important. What is important—I would say crucial—is that *they are the same colors*. If color is light, and light "paints" every object and fills the spectrum with all the colors of nature, and all light colors can be reduced to the three *primary light* colors, we reach the first and most important conclusion concerning color theory and its practical application in painting:

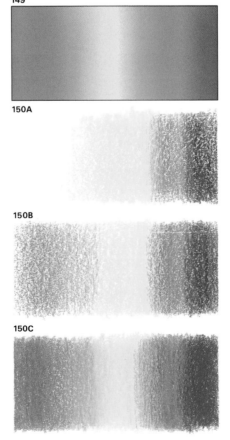

149

150A

150B

150C

**The perfect match between
LIGHT colors and
PIGMENT colors**
enables the artist to
paint all the colors in
nature using only the
three primary pigment colors:
cyan blue, magenta, and yellow.

As an example, I have painted the range of colors of the spectrum (fig. 149) with colored pencils: cyan blue, yellow, and crimson (the latter acting as *magenta*). I began with the blue, darkening the right-hand side with a touch of crimson and blending it with the yellow (fig. 150A). The I used an initial layer of crimson at the left (fig. 150B), finishing by intensifying the crimson and merging it with the yellow. Finally, I made the transition from yellow to green (fig. 150C).

Figs. 149 and 150. The spectrum and a reproduction of it (C) using three colored pencils: crimson, yellow, and blue.

An infinite range of colors using three colors plus black and white

On the first line at right are the three primary pigment colors (A):

Cyan blue
Yellow
Magenta

By mixing these in pairs we can first obtain the secondary colors (B), then the tertiary colors (C), giving us a total of twelve colors (from left to right):

Dark blue
Ultramarine blue
Cyan blue
Emerald green
Green
Light green
Yellow
Orange
Red
Crimson
Magenta
Violet

These twelve colors have maximum *saturating* power; that is, they are pure colors, with no dark or light shades to modify their chromatic essence. See how five lines further down, marked C', these twelve colors are repeated with the same saturation. From that line upwards, the colors become lighter and lighter until they are almost white; moving down from that line, they become progressively darker, down to the last line, which is almost black.

Imagine that instead of just black or white we had mixed each of the colors with yellow, magenta, red, or blue—lighter or darker tones—then we would really have an infinite range of colors.

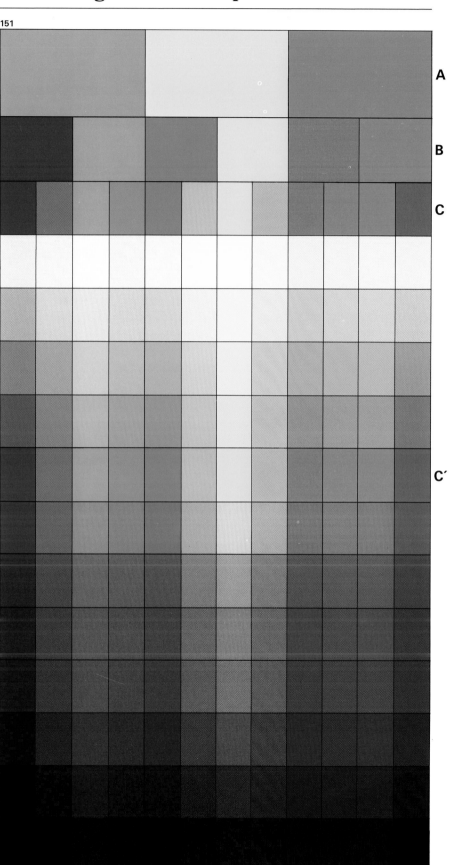

Fig. 151. With the three primary colors mixed in pairs, we obtain the secondary colors which, when mixed with the primaries, produce the tertiary colors. Mixing these with white up to the tertiary colors, and black to the bottom of the diagram, an infinite range of tones and colors can be obtained.

Complementary colors: What are they? How are they used?

Let's return to Young's experiment that reconstructed white light (fig. 154, opposite). In the next figure (155), when the beam of blue light is blocked out, the resulting color is yellow. We can see that the yellow lacks the *complement* of blue to *reconstruct the white light*, and vice versa. Complementing white light with two *light* colors also occurs with the other colors of the spectrum (fig. 156). As our *pigment* colors are the same as the *light* colors, our complementary colors are also the same, but with one basic difference: with *light* colors, when we superimpose colors we are *adding* light together to obtain *white* (fig. 156); with *pigment* colors, when we mix colors we are *subtracting* light, and we get *black* (fig. 157).

COMPLEMENTARY COLORS
(fig. 157)

Yellow is the complementary of **Dark blue**

Magenta is the complementary of **Green**

Cyan blue is the complementary of **Red**

And how are the complementary colors used? First, they are used to produce maximum color contrast when juxtaposed (fig. 152). Second, we use them to paint with a *range of neutral colors* obtained by mixing complementary colors in unequal proportion and adding white (figs. 158 and 159). I shall discuss maxi-mum contrast and neutral colors later on.

Fig. 152. Ernst Ludwig Kirchner (1880–1938), *The Artist and his Model*. Kunsthalle, Hamburg. Kirchner juxtaposes complementary colors in the *fauvist* style.

Fig. 153. The color wheel, with the complementary colors marked by arrows.

Figs. 154 and 155. Projecting the three primary light colors, we obtain white light. But if we block out the blue light, yellow appears; thus, blue is the complementary of yellow.

Figs. 156 and 157. By adding together complementary light colors we obtain white light (fig. 156); by adding the complementary pigment colors, we obtain black (157).

152

153

Figs. 158 and 159. Mixing white with two complementary colors in unequal proportions produces dirty, neutral colors.

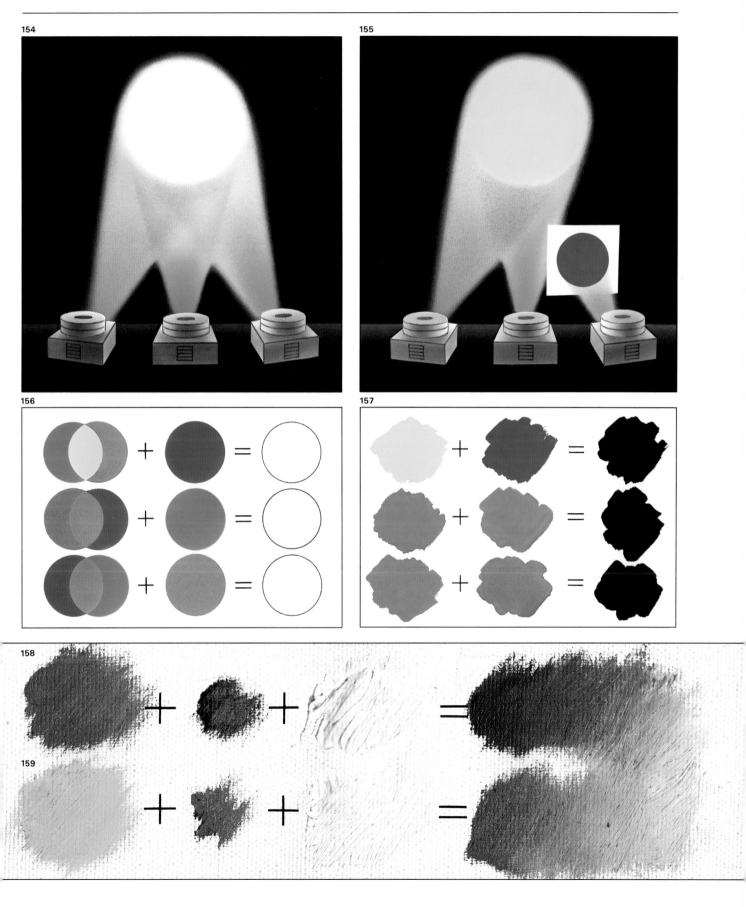

Contrast

Contrast is obtained by comparing two tones or two colors that are notably different from one another. These differences can be minimal or intense, depending on whether the contrast is soft or sharp. Basically, contrasts are either of *tone* or of *color*, although there also exists another type of subjective contrast produced by the eye, called *simultaneous contrast*.

Tonal contrast is characteristic of drawings in lead pencil, charcoal, India ink, and sanguine chalk, as well as watercolors in monochrome gouache (sepia, for example). Tonal contrast also plays a part in oil paintings dominated by form and chiaroscuro.

Color contrast is the comparison of and differences between colors, whether primary or complementary, or between ranges of colors.

Simultaneous contrast is an optical effect in which the contrast between adjacent colors enhances or reduces their saturation.

These are the different types of contrast you should be familiar with:

Tonal contrast

Color contrast

Contrast of range

Complementary contrast

Simultaneous contrast

When we talk about *tonal contrast*, we should distinguish between the terms *tone* and *color*, remembering

Fig. 161. Honoré Daumier (1808–1879), *The Washerwoman*. The Louvre, Paris. This famous painting provides an excellent example of color contrast by tone.

Fig. 162. Gustave Moreau (1826–1898), *The Sirens*. Moreau Museum, Paris. Moreau uses the potential of contrasting ranges of color by placing a warm area within the cool range of the painting.

Fig. 163. Franz von Stuck (1863–1929), *The Kiss of the Sphinx*. The Hermitage, Saint Petersburg. This charcoal drawing is an example of maximum contrast obtained with black and white.

Fig. 160. Francis Picabia (1879–1953), *Catalan Landscape*. Georges Pompidou Center, Paris. An example of color contrast that plays with the juxtaposition of complementary colors.

160

161

162

163

Contrast of tone and color

that light, medium, and dark gray are a range of gray *tones*. In this way, light, medium, and dark blue are a range of blue *tones*, and the same can be said for a range of reds or greens (fig. 164). While juxtaposing yellow, magenta and blue form a range of *colors* that contrast in color. We can then understand why, as a result of the affinity for or predominance of form, when we see a painting by Caravaggio or Velázquez we should think of the dramatic effect or their capacity for expression which results from the contrast of tone. The ability to express ideas or feelings runs parallel to contrasts of tone or color. *Color contrast* can be achieved with a predominance of the primary colors—yellow, magenta, and cyan

blue—remembering that it is also possible to add secondary colors, in addition to black and white. As can be seen in figure 166 and in the reproduction of Botticelli's painting (fig. 167), the result is extremely attractive.

Fig. 164. Tonal contrasts can appear in black, medium gray, and light gray, as well as in colors; for example, medium blue and light blue in blue, or medium green and light green in green. Different *tonalities* within *the same color* are possible, whether in black, blue, ocher, sienna, and so on.

Fig. 165. Edouard Manet (1832–1883), *Ship Setting Sail from Folkestone.* Philadelphia Museum. The famous Impressionist interprets his subject with a predominance of contrasting tones.

Fig. 166. A diagram of color contrasts using the three primary pigment colors, black, and white.

Fig. 167. Sandro Botticelli (1445–1510), *The Burial of Christ* (detail). Pinakothek, Munich. The famous Renaissance painter uses vivid colors to strengthen contrast without juxtaposing complementary colors.

164

166

165

167

Contrast of range

The idea of contrast is usually associated with chiaroscuro and the modeling of forms using the effects of light and shade. But there are other ways to create diversity and variation that are not related to light and shade or to the dramatization of form, but are based instead on the composition and harmony of a painting. These are achieved by creating contrasts with ranges of color. Indeed, if you paint a subject that has a cold tendency (using mostly blues, green, purples, and violets), and in the center or to one side you add a note or a touch of a warm color (such as yellow, ocher, orange, red, magenta, or crimson), you will obtain both a spectacular contrast and a truly creative harmonization of color. The result will be similar to that most spectacular of contrasts: the contrast of complementary colors. Of course, the subject may also have a warm tendency with a cold note added in the center. See this type of contrast in figures 168 to 171, with examples of subjects painted by van Gogh and Mary Cassatt.

Fig. 168. A diagram contrasting warm colors with a grouping of four cold ones.

Fig. 169. Vincent van Gogh (1853–1890), *Making Sheaves* (after a painting by Millet). A good example of the potential of contrasting ranges.

Fig. 170. The warm-colored "note" of ocher-orange, red, orange, and yellow is surrounded by openly cool colors.

Fig. 171. Mary Cassatt (1844–1926), *Girl in a Blue Armchair*. Collection of Mr. and Mrs. Paul Mellon, Upperville, Virginia. "Please, come and sit down here. In this blue armchair." That is probably what the artist thought when she decided to paint this picture. Cassatt saw the group of blue armchairs and imagined the girl with her white dress and the flesh color of the face, arms, and legs—a group of warm colors—surrounded by cool blue tones.

169

168

170

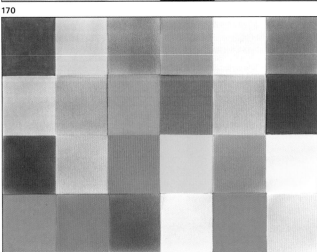

171

Contrast of complementary colors

Contrasts of complementary colors are the most violent and spectacular (fig. 172):

Cyan blue against **Red**
Magenta against **Green**
Yellow against **Dark blue**

In one of his letters to his brother Theo, van Gogh made a concise and astute comment about the subject of complementary colors:

"If complementary colors of equal value are used—that is, of the same degree of vividness and light—when juxtaposed they will be of such violent intensity that the human eye could scarcely bear the sight."

This definition may sound like an exaggeration to anyone who is not a painter, or to anyone who is not van Gogh himself, an artist of fire and passion. But van Gogh's comment coincides with the fact that juxtaposing complementary colors creates the most spectacular of contrasts. Matisse, Derain, Vlaminck, Kandinsky, and so on, of whom van Gogh was a predecessor, used the contrast of complementary colors in order to exalt light and color. And they were called the *fauves* ("wild beasts") because of their achievements with those "violent contrasts" in their use of complementary colors.

On this page you can see the painting *Bonnard in his Studio* by Edouard Vuillard, the famous postimpressionist painter, a painter of everyday household scenes. Vuillard always painted with ranges of neutral colors.

Fig. 172. This is the pattern of contrasts between complementary colors, providing maximum contrast when juxtaposing

A Cyan blue - B Red
C Magenta - D Green
E Yellow - F Dark blue

Fig. 173. Maurice Vlaminck (1878–1958), *Tugboat on Chatou*. Chicago Art Institute. This painting is typical of the work of the fauvists, who produced spectacular contrasts in their paintings by juxtaposing complementary colors.

Fig. 174. Edouard Vuillard (1868–1940), *Sketch for Bonnard's Portrait*. Museum of Modern Art, Paris. As was mentioned earlier, mixing complementary colors with white is the basis for the ranges of neutral colors, which were used by the artist in this painting.

173

172

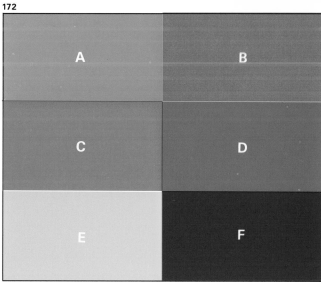

174

Simultaneous contrast

There are two "classic" ways of beginning to paint a picture: The first and easiest is the one recommended by Camille Corot when he asserted that "the first thing to finish is the drawing, then the values, and then the color." The other formula, advocated by the impressionist Alfred Sisley, was "I always begin a painting with the sky," a statement which, when you think of the space taken up by the sky, is equivalent to saying *"I always begin a painting by filling spaces."*

"What spaces?" you may ask. When you begin a painting by starting with an object or a small area and then move on to the background, the color of the object or area may well be altered by the effect of *simultaneous contrast*. Leonardo da Vinci first wrote about simultaneous contrast in his *Treatise on Painting*: "Black clothes make the flesh look whiter. Whites, on the other hand, darken its color"; a perception confirmed by Michel-Eugène Chevreul in 1839, who established this law by conducting the following experiment:

Place two sheets of paper of the same size next to each other on a table, one black and one white. Then place a small white square in the center of the black sheet. You will see that the white square *looks whiter* than the larger sheet. Now make two cutouts of gray paper the same size as the smaller square, and place one of these cutouts on the white paper and the other on the sheet of black paper. Now you are able to see, as Leonardo said, that "black clothes make the flesh (the gray) look whiter. Whites, on the other hand, darken its color."

The law of simultaneous contrasts is as follows:

- **White appears whiter the darker the surrounding tone**

- **Gray is more intense the lighter the surrounding tone (figs. 176 and 177)**

- **A color can be lighter or darker, depending on the surrounding tone or color (figs. 178 to 181A)**

One of the most convincing examples of this law can been seen in figure 175. At first glance it seems obvious that the narrow stripe dividing the gray-blue gradation is lighter on the left-hand side and darker on the right. But if you cover the areas above and below the stripe with white paper, you will be surprised to find that the gray-blue of the stripe is the same even tone along its entire length.

Fig. 175. An interesting optical effect caused by *simultaneous contrast:* The center stripe seems to lighten from left to right, but if you cover the gradated areas above and below you will be surprised to see that the stripe is one uniform gray color.

Figs. 176 and 177. The two figures possess the same tonal value but, because of the change in background due to the effect of *simultaneous contrast*, the figure seems darker against the white background and lighter against the black background.

Figs. 178 to 181A. In accordance with the *law of simultaneous contrast*, color chips on a white background look darker and more intense than those on a black background.

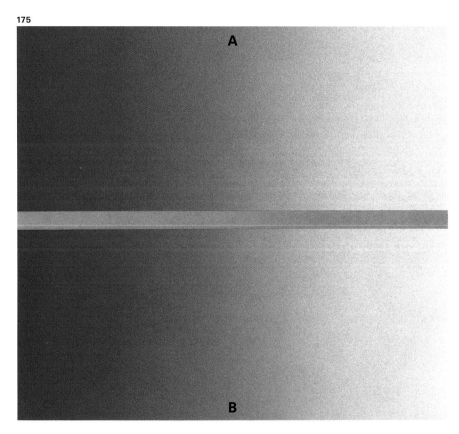

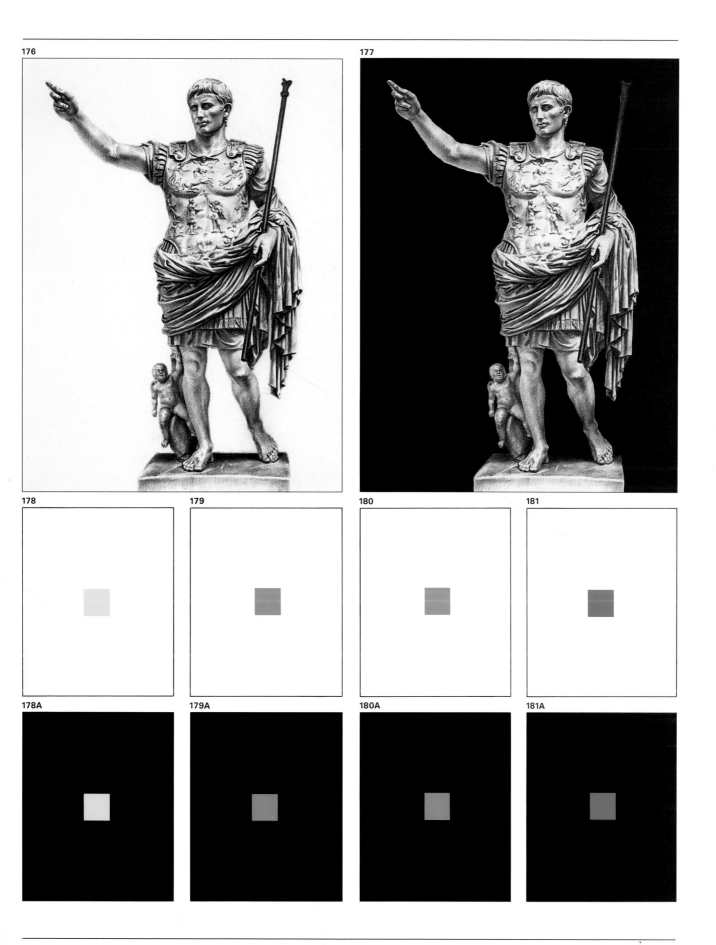

176

177

178

179

180

181

178A

179A

180A

181A

Effect of complementary colors

182

183

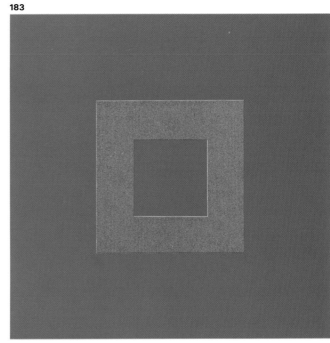

184

The effect of complementary colors is a phenomenon produced by simultaneous contrast, resulting from the fact that when we see a particular color, we also need to see the complementary color simultaneously.

You can confirm this yourself by looking at the gray square on the yellow background in figure 182 for twenty or thirty seconds. You will find that the gray square shows a clear tendency toward yellow's complementary, which is dark blue. You can also test this effect with figure 183, where the gray square shows a certain tendency to the complementary of dark blue, which is yellow. Also on the subject of simultaneous contrast, figure 184 illustrates the rule that *the juxtaposition of the same color in different tonalities enhances tones, lightening the lighter tones and darkening the darker ones.*

Returning to the effect of complementary colors, you can now experience also the phenomenon of *afterimages* (fig. 185, opposite). Under a good light, stare for at least thirty seconds at the three leaves in primary colors, concentrating your gaze on the yellow leaf in the middle. Then look toward the center of the white space above, and you will see another three leaves floating above the first set, in their complementary colors, which will be clear, luminous, and rather fluorescent.

Figs. 182 and 183. The two gray squares are identical in tone, but if you stare for about thirty seconds at the gray square on the yellow background, the gray will eventually take on a pronounced bluish cast. When you stare at the set of squares on the right, you will see that the gray square against the dark blue background tends toward yellow. This phenomenon is called the *effect of complementary colors.*

Figs. 184 and 184A. Notice how the same tone (A) becomes lighter or darker when juxtaposed against a progressive scale of varying tones.

184A

Successive images

Fig. 185. Here you can see the optical effect of *successive images*. Under a bright light, stare for at least thirty seconds at the three leaves printed in magenta, yellow, and cyan blue. Then look up toward the center of the white space, and you will see a "ghosted" version of the three leaves in their complementary colors, which are luminous and fluorescent.

From all we have said so far about the contrast of complementary colors and simultaneous contrast, we can draw a practical conclusion:

The enhancement of complementary colors—their tone and color—when they are juxtaposed, and the phenomenon of successive images, including the maximum color contrast that complementary colors can provide, lead us to conclude that the sight of any color creates, by "sympathy," the appearance of its complementary in the surrounding color. The famous color physicist Chevreul discovered and established this fact as a theoretical and practical rule in the following words:

"To place a brushstroke of color on a canvas is not only to stain the canvas with the color on the paint brush. It also means to cast over the surrounding space its complementary color."

The effect of complementary colors in practice

We are going to study the theory of simultaneous contrast and the effect of complementary colors from a practical point of view.

This study of the effect of complementary colors uses a magnificent painting by the well-known artist Badia Camps, reproduced on this page (fig. 186). We extend our gratitude to the artist for allowing this study and his work to be reproduced. I would also like to point out that the colored backgrounds created for Badia Camps's original are no more than studio experiments that I have carried out in order to illustrate the theory of the effect of complementary colors. Moreover, I would like to stress that these color tests were carried out on much bigger enlargements, in which the effect was more noticeable than in these smaller reproductions.

Figure 187: Over a reproduction of a painting by Badia Camps, I have painted a yellow background that, through the effect of complementary colors, lends a slightly bluish tendency to the figure. The yellow background that induces the dark blue cast underlines the contrast and the gray-green flesh color of the original figure painted by the artist.

Figure 188: The background is now a dark magenta color that, due to its intensity, eliminates or reduces the contrast of the original painting while highlighting the intensity of the flesh color by producing green, the complementary color of magenta.

Figure 189: A cyan blue background creates the complementary red, which dirties the neutral color of the original figure.

Let us now analyze the original painting (figure 186). Badia Camps painted this figure with a neutral,

186

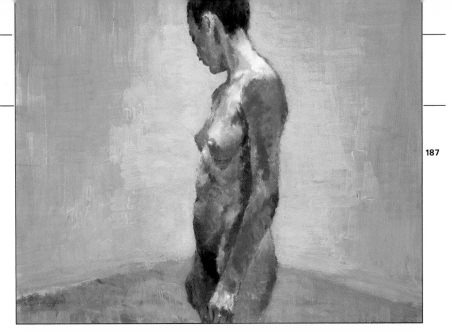

gray background, a slightly warm gray that matches the neutral yellow ground and the neutral gray-green flesh color, reminiscent of Delacroix when he said: "Give me mud and I will paint the skin of Venus... provided I can paint around her the colors I want."

As a final comment on the subject of contrasts, notice how Badia Camps highlights the figure in relation to the background by using what I call *created contrasts:* In this example, lightening the background to the left of the figure, darkening it behind the neck, lightening it toward the lower, a technique used by both the great masters and present-day artists.

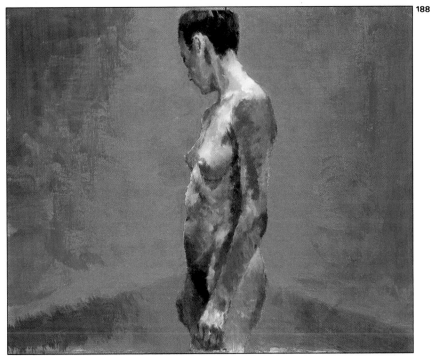

188

Figs. 186 to 189. Using a splendid painting by the artist Badia Camps, I have modified the backgrounds of three copies, one with yellow, another with magenta, and a third with cyan blue, (fig. 187, 188, and 189). Due to the *effect of complementary colors*, the figure against the yellow background takes on a bluish cast, against the magenta background a greenish hue, and against the cyan blue background a reddish tendency. This is consistent with the rule formulated by Chevreul: "To paint any color on a surface is to color the surrounding area with its complementary color."

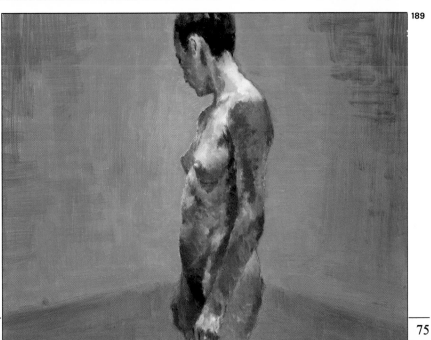

189

Having examined some theory, it's time get down to the practical side. First we will analyze the colors of objects in order to better understand the concept of color. Such a study must always consider the three factors that affect an object's color—local color, tonal color, and reflected color—and that color depends on the color of the light. Distance is also an important factor in the perception of color, because it affects color and determines contrasts between planes. For that reason we talk about near and distant color. Finally, we will look at the effects of white and black when mixed with other colors, to prevent you from falling into the "gray trap," as so many other painters do.

THE COLOR OF OBJECTS

Local color

Fig. 191. This polyhedron is lit from the front, which barely creates any shadows. It is highlighted by its *local color*, or the color of the object itself, which is white.

The color of objects is determined by the following basic factors:

a) *The local color*

b) *The tonal color (resulting from the effects of light and shadow)*

c) *The reflected color*

d) *The color of the intervening atmosphere*

There is not much to say about local color, which is the object's own color: for instance, the red of a tomato, the yellow of a lemon, or the green of an apple. Local color always exists, although it is more evident when an object is lit from the front (fig. 193).

Manet was the first artist to resolve his pictures exclusively with local color (refer to *The Fifer*, fig. 192). This approach largely predominated in the impressionist movement, and later on was used by the *fauves*, who painted with flat, saturated *local colors*.

Delacroix said: "Real painters don't paint only with local color." In accordance with this recommendation van Gogh wrote: "I study the colors of nature so as not to paint senseless colors. But I'm not worried if my color is not identical, as long as it appears beautiful in my picture." Take note of these artists' words. It's all a question of looking at the object's color and then interpreting it.

Fig. 192. Édouard Manet (1832–1883), *The Fifer*. This painting established the criteria of the impressionist movement: painting with flat colors, depicting very few any shadows, and *highlighting objects with their own color*. This required the use of a bright palette.

Fig. 193. A graphic representation of what is meant by the term *local color*, or color of the object itself: the red of the tomato, the yellow of the lemon, and so on.

Tonal color

Fig. 194. This is the same polyhedron as appears on the previous page, only here it is illuminated laterally, which produces a number of planes in shadow. This effect allows us to observe *local color:* a series of varying tones of the object's own color.

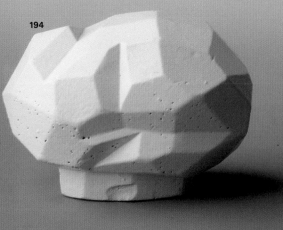

When the direction of light changes from frontal to lateral, an object's *tonal color* is emphasized, promoted by the effects of light and shadow (fig. 194). The white polyhedron's parts are darker or lighter, some because they receive a stronger intensity of light, and others because they are to a greater or lesser extent at opposite points with respect to the direction of the light.

In the preceding image there is only one light source illuminating the polyhedron, so there are only two hues corresponding to the local color (white) and the tonal color (gray). This is an exceptional case, because generally the tonal color is influenced by reflected colors. For example, you can see the yellow of the lemon in the red tomato, and the green of the apple in the lemon's tonal color. We could sum up thus:

Tonal color is a variation of the local color, usually influenced by the reflection of the colors of other objects.

Figs. 195 and 196. Camille Pissarro's *Self-Portrait* and Cézanne's *Self-Portrait*, both in the Musée d'Orsay, Paris, are good graphic examples of the use of local and tonal colors.

Fig. 197. Here the tomato, lemon, and apple continue to reflect their local color on their illuminated side, but their tonal color can be observed in their parts in shadow.

Reflected color

Fig. 198. This polyhedron is also illuminated laterally, but the yellow card placed at right produces *reflected light*.

198

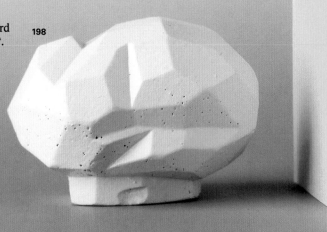

199

The white polyhedron and the piece of yellow cardboard are lit laterally from the left. The light that reaches the cardboard is bounced off and reflected onto the portion of the polyhedron in shadow, and the reflected light is so strong that it practically eliminates the polyhedron's tonal color. However, such a strong reflection also destroys the polyhedron's shape. Ingres advised his students thus: "Avoid using too many reflections, since they will destroy the form."

The use of reflected light is not always advisable, and in certain instances it can be totally counterproductive. However, in small quantities it does help to enhance the form of an object, as can be seen in the colors reflected by the blue and red cards onto the lemon and apple in figure 200.

On the other hand, reflected light can act as a source of complementary light. This is possible in the majority of cases in which the subject is backlit, such as in the self-portrait of Cézanne on the previous page, in figure 196. In this example, the painter's face was created using reflected light. We can see a similar approach in Renoir's painting *Woman Reading* (fig. 199): here, the artist has used light reflected from the pages of the book the woman is reading.

Fig. 199. Pierre Auguste Renoir (1841–1919), *Woman Reading*. Musée d'Orsay, Paris. In this painting, Renoir used a "trick of the trade" by illuminating the model's face with light reflected from the pages of a book.

Fig. 200. Light reflected from the colored cards produces a green reflection on the lemon and a red one on the apple.

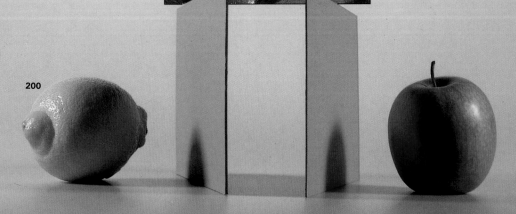

200

The color and intensity of light

201

202

When the white polyhedron is illuminated by a yellow and a blue light, it takes on the color of the lights (fig. 201). The red tomato looks almost black when illuminated by its complementary color, green (fig. 203A); the yellow lemon acquires a reddish color under a soft violet light (fig. 203B); the green apple looks brown when illuminated by an orange light (fig. 203C).

The color of objects changes according to the color and intensity of light. Natural light is blue; artificial light is normally yellow. The light of northern countries is "cold"; in the south it is "warmer," more golden. Of course, a good painter is normally attuned to such tendencies and takes advantage of them—even to the point of exaggeration—in order to achieve a more artistic vision of the subject.

In sunlight or full light colors become saturated; they are totally reflective. When the light decreases, the colors also decrease in intensity. The total absence of light produces black, but a reduction in light does not suppose a blackening of colors, it simply leads to a more bluish type of light that impregnates all colors with blue.

Fig. 201. When the color of the light changes, so does the color of the object. Logically, if the polyhedron is illuminated by a blue light on one side and a yellow one on the other, shades of these two colors will be produced, even mixed together, on the polyhedron.

Fig. 202. When we paint at five o'clock in the afternoon while the sun is low, the colors take on a warm tendency, as we can see in this detail of my painting, *Street at Dusk* (private collection).

Fig. 203 A to C. The color of a light source can alter the color of an object, as we can see here: The red tomato illuminated by a green light looks black, and so on.

203A

203B

203C

The color of the intervening atmosphere

204

"...and the fields appear to be bluer, the farther they are from the eye." Leonardo da Vinci had already discovered this more than five hundred years ago. It is not necessary to be a painter or artist to perceive that the most distant parts of a landscape—whether trees, houses, or fields—take on violet-blue and grayish tones because of the effect of the intervening color of the atmosphere. The farther away the objects, the lighter their tones. As a good painter, you must be capable of capturing and painting this type of atmosphere and others (fig. 204).

As a painter and sensitive artist, you *must attempt to see and find* ("I don't search, I find," said Picasso) a type of atmosphere whose perception is out of the average person's range. We are talking about the *back-lighting effect*.

You are undoubtedly familiar with it. Imagine you are walking through the country on a road that leads toward a mountain, with the sun on the right. It is about half past ten in the morning, so the sun is still low. Suddenly the road winds to the right, and the sun is now shining in your face: This is the back-lighting effect. The mountain in the distance has taken on a blue-gray color, and there is a misty halo between the mountain and the trees and shrubs that remain in the shade, while the road and the grass reflect the sun's color and light (fig. 206). The very same effect can occur on water, at a marina full of boats in the morning before the sun reaches its zenith. You get a back-lighting effect that colors the marina in shades of gold. Back-lighting is very often experienced when it is least expected; for example, when turning a street corner (fig. 205).

One more thing: The atmosphere, that intervening space that Leonardo called *aerial perspective*, is something that the artist and

Fig. 204. A graphic representation of intervening atmosphere, a phenomenon that transforms the color, contrast, and definition of objects the farther away they are from the viewer. An example of this effect can be seen in the lack of color intensity of distant mountains.

Fig. 205. José M. Parramón, *San Augustín Square* (detail). Private collection. The back-lighting effect produces the effect of intervening atmosphere, which enhances the color of the subject.

206

painter must always interpret, even when the subject of a drawing or painting lacks the depth of many planes, such as a still life, a portrait, or a nude. It's simply a question of defining the very first plane with the greatest precision. It is the nose in a portrait, or the nearest apple in a still life. Then something must be left a little fuzzy, somewhat out of focus. This is the middle ground: the ears or the hair in a portrait, or whatever is behind the apple in the still life. As Leonardo said, "successive planes become more vaporous and less precise in the distance."

Fig. 206. José M. Parramón, *Bellver in Winter* (detail). Private collection. It is easy to see the back-lighting effect in this country scene. The resulting intervening atmospheric effect allows us to express depth.

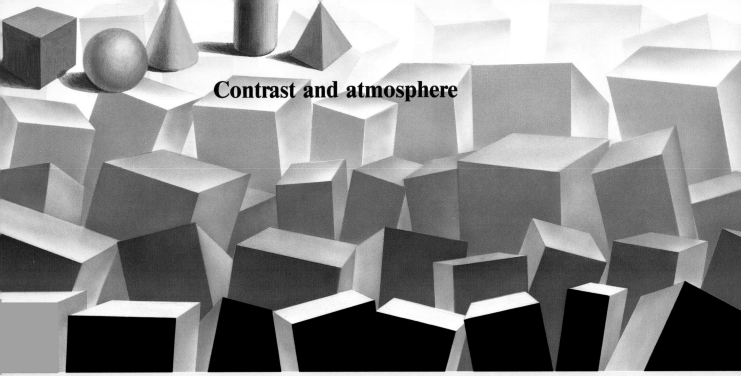

207

Contrast and atmosphere

It is said that when Titian left a painting of Pope Paul III on his balcony to dry passersby believed it was the Pope himself.

Titian must have been proud of his achievement: painting a two-dimensional image with such realism that the people on the street could see the third dimension in it.

In order to represent depth in a picture we must remember these four factors:

FACTORS FOR REPRESENTING THE THIRD DIMENSION

* *Lineal perspective*: A series of parallel or oblique lines that converge at the horizon.
* *Form*: Created by the effects of light and shadow; the chiaroscuro of objects.
* *Contrast*: Sharpness in the foreground and a softening of the receding planes.
* *Intervening atmosphere*: Differing intensities of color combined with contrast between the foreground and the background.

Let's leave the subject of perspective for the moment and concentrate on the title of this page: *Contrast and atmosphere*. In regard to this matter, the German philosopher Hegel compared the qualities and virtues of architecture, sculpture, painting, and music in his *System of Arts*. When discussing the "character of painting," Hegel came to several conclusions about contrast and atmosphere, which in my opinion are definitive:

"According to the intervening atmosphere, in the real world all objects undergo a slight change in color. The color or tone that is erased by distance is known as *aerial perspective*. It is also responsible for the change in the object's contours and tones."

Leonardo da Vinci had already advanced this idea, but it was Hegel who confirmed it. Hegel also considered the representation of the effects of contrast and atmosphere; that is, the third dimension.

"The layman believes that the foreground is lighter and the background is darker. This is not so.

In reality, the foreground is darker and lighter at the same time;

however, the contrast of light and shadows is more intense the nearer the object is to the painter, and at the same time the contours are sharper." To underline this Hegel added:

"The farther away objects are, the more they fade and lose their form, because the contrast between light and shadow gradually disappears."

208

209

210

Figs. 207 to 210. The images reproduced on these pages are all examples of the fundamental laws of contrast and depth, which an artist must take into account. Hegel summed up these laws in his *System of Arts:* (1) The foreground of a subject is darker and lighter at the same time, and (2) the more distant an object, the less intense its color. These factors can be appreciated in real images, such as the photograph at left (fig. 210), in the plan and picture I painted of the port of Barcelona (figs. 208 and 209), and in the image at the top of page 84 (fig. 207).

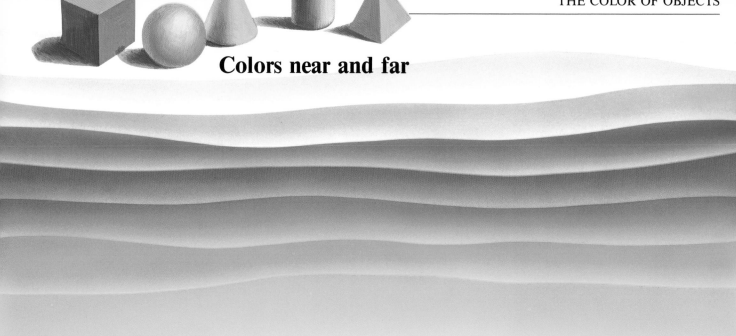

Colors near and far

211

There are colors that "bring objects, planes, and masses closer," and colors that "distance" them. If we compose a painting in which the foreground is yellow, the next plane orange, and the succeeding ones red, green, blue, and blue-gray, we obtain a perfect three-dimensional representation (fig. 211). This is due to *color contrast*, since yellow is the brightest color (after white), followed by orange, red, and so on, until we reach the blues, which end in the diffuse, bluish-gray of the distant atmosphere. You may say that such a landscape cannot be easily found. This is true, but all you have to do is find an ocher or yellow wheat field or a light earth-colored field for the foreground, wait for the light to reach the right point, and observe the blue or blue-gray effect of the intervening atmosphere. It's simply a question of knowing where to find it and use it in a painting.

There other subjects that allow you more control than a landscape. The still life is a case in point. It gives you total freedom to arrange and compose your objects. For example, in the foreground you could place an apple, some bananas, and grapes—all yellow in color—or a yellow ceramic pot; in the middle ground, some red and green vegetables. All that is left is to paint a blue or gray background.

212

Finally, *you can interpret* not only forms but also colors by
> *changing,*
> *accentuating,*
> *omitting,*
> *adding,*
> *intensifying....*

Figs. 211 and 212. "Yellow nears and light blue distances." Of course, it is not essential, but you should remember this when you are looking for a subject to paint and take it into account when representing depth. If you also clearly define objects in the foreground and soften forms in the background, you are on the road to achieving a good painting.

The gray trap

Mari Paz sets up her easel and arranges her oil colors. She will use a No. 15 landscape canvas. This is the third time that Mari Paz has painted in the country. First she sketches the basic forms in charcoal, then proceeds to paint. "I'll start with the sky," thinks Mari Paz. Someone told her that the sky is not simply blue and white, but that in its upper reaches she should mix a little carmine with the blue, and in the lower sky she should add more white and a little yellow. She faithfully follows this advice. Mari Paz paints the upper area with blue, carmine, and white, and adds a small quantity of yellow below. She then returns to the upper area to touch up the sky. The sky is now finished, although it does look a little gray. Now for the

trees. Mari Paz thinks aloud as she mixes her colors in an attempt to find the colors closest to that of the trees: "...green, a little sienna, a little blue, some white...in the light of the trunk, more white....More light, more whites [this is pure logic for Mari Paz], some more blue and sienna for the parts in shadow...or maybe it would be better to add a little burnt umber." Mari Paz paints the earth and dirt road with a light brown and mixes burnt umber with white. The result is a light coffee color, so she adds a tiny amount of blue and carmine to the mix. Mari Paz contemplates her picture. She is not at all pleased with it. It is rather colorless— it's all gray.

If I had been with Mari

Paz, I would have told her that before touching up the top part of the sky she should clean her brush first, because when going from yellow to blue with a little carmine and a lot of white, the only thing that will happen is that you will fall into a trap, "the gray trap." I would have explained to Mari Paz that a mix of blue and burnt umber produces black or a dark brown. If she had incorporated a little white, she would have gotten a wonderful gray. The most important thing I would have said to Mari Paz is that you do not only use white and black to lighten and darken objects.

But allow me to look at this problem on the following page.

213

The use and abuse of white

You already know that when you mix the three primary colors—cyan blue, magenta, and yellow—you get black. You also know that when mixing equal amounts of two complementaries—green and purple, dark blue and yellow, or cyan blue and red—you also get black. When you add white to these equal color mixes you get a darker or lighter gray, depending on how much white you add. If you abuse white and use it exclusively to lighten colors, you will fall into the "gray trap." This is because white will turn gray; do not forget that gray is obtained by mixing white and black. If you have some experience with watercolors, you will know that there is no white watercolor pigment: since watercolors are transparent, the white is the white of the paper. So if you want to paint a light watercolor sepia, you must add more and more water to the dark sepia to make it more transparent so that the white of the paper will show through. But white does exist as a color in oil paints. If you mix white with the same sepia to obtain a brighter tone, the sepia will become gray and dirty looking, losing its brightness.

Fig. 214. If you pour a little coffee into two glasses and gradually add water to one of them and milk to the other, you will to see how the water lightens the color without changing its hue, while the milk clouds and changes the color of the coffee by "graying" its original hue. This is similar to what happens when we lighten a transparent color (watercolor) and when we lighten an opaque color (oil) with white.

We can prove this with a practical experiment. Do you like coffee? Black or "white," with cream? I drink it black and you—if you would be so kind—will have it with milk. We are in the café on the corner. I've ordered two cups of coffee in big glasses, with a jug of water and a jug of milk. Note that the color of the coffee is identical in both glasses, a dark sienna that is almost black. We will lighten this dark color; I will use water and you will use the milk.

Ready? In my glass the tone has changed very little, but the color of your coffee has changed entirely. It's now paler, more cloudy and grayish. The more water and milk I add to my coffee, the lighter it becomes: first a reddish shade of sienna, then a color similar to wine, then a golden yellow. In your glass, the cloudy sienna becomes a light earth color, then a light beige, a gray meat color, and finally a light gray. This experiment shows the difference between painting with transparent and opaque colors, and can be summed up with the words of the impressionist painter Degas:

"Never trust the color white."

Fig. 215. Because this still life is lit from the front there are practically no effects of light and shadow. It is for this same reason that I resolved this picture with flat colors, with almost no white, an excellent way to avoid what I call the "gray trap."

215

What can be said about the use of black?

Black was the first pigment color, and was the primary pigment color of the Egyptians, Greeks, and Romans. Black was also used during the Renaissance and Baroque periods. Rubens painted his pictures on a previously applied coat of silver grays, first drawing the subject with blacks and black browns and highlighting them with white. Velázquez painted directly on the canvas without drawing the subject first, applying a general impression of the colors in which gray predominated (Velázquez's famous grisaille). Most of the romantic painters of the nineteenth century used *bitumen*, a dark brown pigment made from asphalt.

The impressionists (Manet, Monet, Pissarro, Cézanne, and Degas, among others) discovered *open-air painting*. They renounced black, removed it from their palettes, and painted the shadows in blue and complementary colors.

Then came the post-impressionists, *fauves*, cubists, surrealists, and so on, and with them black returned to the palette and the picture. In a letter to his brother Theo, van Gogh defended the use of black, but only under certain conditions: "One does not have to be against black. All colors can be used in a picture on the one condition that they find their place in the picture and are in harmony with the others."

To this I would add what Degas said—"Never trust the color white"—but apply it to black. Although black as a local color—for example, a black dress—is totally acceptable, you should

NEVER use black as a tonal color.

Black mixed with other colors is extremely dangerous: it grays, dirties, and alters tone. If you need to confirm this theory, just look at the example of the use and abuse of black (fig. 216) and compare it with the same subject, painted in the objects' real colors (fig. 217). In the figure at

216

217

top the poorness of the color is evident, especially the color of the shadows, which gray and dirty the blue jug, turn the apple's yellow into green, and alter the red of the pepper, thus losing its chromatic identity. Now look at the figure below and observe the richness of color and the transparency of the shadows, as well as the realistic quality of the high-

lights. This has been achieved by eliminating black and controlling the white. To avoid the results shown in figure 216, we must imitate the colors of nature, as well as the mixes and transitions created by the effects of light. The solution can always be found in the spectrum. In the case of yellow, for example, we can see in the spectrum (fig. 218) that darkness originates from the reds. Red is the first color, which then becomes orange, then yellow, until it merges with green and blue. Therefore, the perfect range of a gradated yellow must begin with black, followed by violet-red, English red, orange, cadmium yellow medium, lemon yellow, and finally white. Figures 220 to 224 illustrate gradated red and blue, darkened only with black and lightened with white (BAD), compared with the results obtained from doing it with the appropriate spectral range (GOOD).

Black alone cannot represent a lack of light.

Here are three classic formulas to compose black without using black:

Formula A—Neutral black
1 part burnt umber
1 part emerald green
1 part 1 part deep madder

Formula B—Warm black
1 part deep madder
1 part burnt umber
1/2 part emerald green

Formula C—Cool black
1 part burnt umber
1 part Prussian blue
1/2 part emerald green

"Warm black" has a reddish tendency, and is appropriate for painting the black of a door or the window of a building in the sun. "Cool black" has a bluish tendency, and can be used to paint the black of a very dark area in the middle of a forest.

Figs. 216 and 217. (Opposite page) The use and abuse of color can lead to the problems illustrated in figure 216, in which poor, dirty colors represent the objects' real colors. In figure 217 the black has been eliminated and the use of white has been controlled, thus achieving a notable color enhancement and an improved representation of reality.

Figs. 218 to 224. Here you can see how to darken and lighten colors by referring to the painted spectrum (fig. 218). Compare the results obtained with yellow (figs. 221 and 222) and red (figs. 223 and 224), when the entire spectrum is used to darken and lighten them, instead of only black and white.

225

The answer to the problem of painting the color of shadows, regardless of the color of the light, is the starting point for this chapter, in which color is studied from a practical point of view. Following a step-by-step sequence the same subject is painted in two contrasting styles: a *value* style and a *colorist's* style. The manufacture and characteristics of the pigments used by professionals are also covered, as well as everything you need know about the variety, quality, and permanence of pigment colors.

LIGHT, SHADOW, AND COLOR

The color of shadows

From the time of Giotto, Leonardo, Raphael, and Titian through nineteenth century, almost every painter would paint a shadow's tone by darkening an object's local color. This technique was more widely used by some artists than others. For example, the *Tenebrists*, led by Caravaggio, would instead paint the shadows of flesh colors with very dark brown; Rubens, on the other hand, would represent the shadows of his models with more luminous colors, such as reddish siennas, golden hues, and ochers. Caravaggio's influence can be seen particularly in Velázquez's early work, and later on in the work of Titian and Rubens. Although he continued to paint the tone of the shadows with a darker local color, Caravaggio began to use grayish hues in his work, composed of a mixture of dark browns, black, and white. But the nineteenth century also felt the influence of the impressionists, who worked outdoors in natural light; with the light came the blue of the shadows: ''I continually search for the blue in shadows'' (van Gogh). Impressionism brought with it, as you know, the color theories of Michel-Eugène Chevreul, who proposed that the complementary color of an object's local color was part of the color of its shadow.

Thanks to Chevreul and the impressionists' experiments we now know which colors to use to paint shadows:

1. **the blue present in all shadows,** mixed with

2. **the local color in a darker tone,** mixed with

3. **the complementary color, in each case, of the local color.**

We are now going to try this out. I am going to paint the subject in figure 226 first, only in blue (fig. 229). Then I shall paint the same subject again, but this time I will depict the tonality of the shadows in a darker local color (fig. 230). Then I shall paint a

third version, and include the complementary color of the local tones of each object in shadow (fig. 233, on page 96). I shall then paint the subject a fourth time, using a mixture of the three previous colors for the shadows: blue, the darker local color, and its complementary (fig. 235, on page 97).

A shadow's main color: blue
When we discussed the color of objects and the intensity of the light (page 81), we said that the reduction of light results in a bluish light that shrouds all objects in blue. You need only see a landscape at dusk to see that *everything looks blue* (fig. 228).

Fig. 226. Here is the subject and setup I have chosen in order to demonstrate the theory that three colors make up the color of shadows: blue, the local color in a darker tone, and the complementary color of the local color.

For the same reason, because there is less light in shadow, even in broad daylight, blue is present in its color (fig. 227).

See how much blue has been used to reproduce the subject in figure 229; notice that even the white of the tablecloth has a certain blue color. Think about this and remember it: *in principle, shadows are blue.*

229

230

Figs. 227 and 228. (Opposite page) Two examples that demonstrate that blue is present in the color of shadows, which becomes obvious when viewed in photographs taken in broad daylight and at dusk.

Figs. 229 and 230. Note the density of the blue in the shadows of the subject painted only in that color, and compare it with the same subject painted in local colors with darker shades of those same colors in the areas in shadow.

231

232

A shadow's second color: its local color

Using the local color *in a darker tone* I have painted a second version of the subject (fig. 230), darkening the red apples with crimson, the yellow apples with red, and the orange with a reddish sienna. The darker local color gives the fruit a rounded form but doesn't quite capture the color of the shadow due to the lack of blue and, in each case, of the complementary to the local color.

Figs. 231 and 232. Basic colors used for the main color (blue) and the darker tones of the local colors (raw umber and cadmium lemon yellow) in the still life above.

A shadow's third color: the complementary of the local color

233

234

The *fauves* painted this way: André Derain painted his famous *Portrait of Matisse* using orange to illuminate the face on one side and green on the side in shadow. Matisse, in turn, painted a portrait of Derain, and also used green for the parts in shadow. The complementary color is always present in the color of the shadow. If you paint a treetop with green and you mix, for the part in shadow, the green with crimson—its complementary color—you will see a perfect relationship between the color of the illuminated parts and the parts in shadow. If, in the same landscape, you paint the earth color of a sunny lane and where a few trees or a fence cast their shadows you mix some Prussian blue, white, and crimson—bluish violet, the complementary color of the earth color—you will obtain an almost perfect shadow color. Then it is a matter of modifying it slightly, perhaps with a touch more crimson here, or white or ocher there. This is because these mixtures are obviously not mathematical, for the blue present in all shadows and the darker tone of the local color (the second formula) as well as the complementary color of the local color may be more or less intense, lighter or darker, tending toward one color or another. But the formula itself holds true: Put it into practice and remember to use it.

The final result

Yes, this is the finished painting, or rather a reproduction of the finished painting. The real picture is twice the size, and though the colors are the same the hues can be seen more clearly in the original. Even so, I believe you can see how blue is used in the shadows, for example, in the shadows of the tablecloth, in the light reflected by the orange, in the yellow apples. You can also see the local color in a darker tone in these apples, as well as a visible hue in the shadow of the fruit bowl. And as for the complementary colors, they can be seen in all of the fruits, especially the red apples and the orange, as well as the yellow apples, which have a slightly violet tinge resulting from the mixture of the blue of the shadow, the red of the darker local color, and

the violet-blue as its complement. Finally, notice how a warm black color has been obtained in the shadows of the red apples by mixing green, crimson, and blue, one of the formulas we have studied here when discussing the use of black.

Fig. 233. Here I have painted the subject's shadows in the complementary colors of its objects' local colors; for example, blue in the shadow of the yellow apple, and green in the shadow of the red apple.

Fig. 234. Two of the complementary colors used to complete the shadows' third colors.

Fig. 235. The finished painting.

Fig. 236. When completing the final details, all of the complementary colors are added.

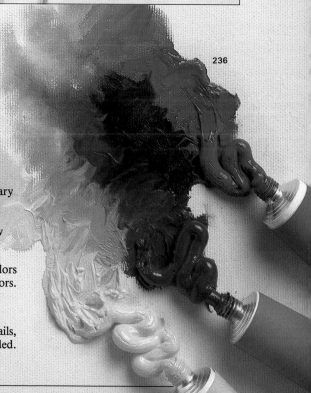

Value painting

237

238

239

240

Fig. 237. In order to express values in my painting, I have illuminated this still life laterally.

Figs. 238 to 240. First, I sketch the subject in charcoal, working out the objects' shadows from the beginning. I then apply a fixative so that the charcoal will not dirty the colors when I paint over the sketch. Then I "fill spaces" in order to eliminate the white of the canvas and thus avoid the effect of simultaneous contrast.

The term *value painting* means painting all the values of a color, all the variations of chiaroscuro, expressing the entire play of light and shadow. *Colorist painting*, on the other hand, means to paint with flat, saturated colors, without expressing shadows. Most of the old masters (Leonardo da Vinci, Titian, Velázquez, Delacroix, and so forth) are *value* painters. Many modern and contemporary artists such as Degas, Sargent, Dalí, and even the early Picasso are *value* painters. *Colorist painting* began with the *fauves:* Matisse, Derain, Vlaminck, and so on. So as to better understand the techniques and styles of value painters and colorists, I will explain the characteristics of each by painting the same still life, showing both images as they are completed, step-by-step. You should also try this experiment by composing your subject and painting it twice, once in each style.

The first condition necessary for *value* painting is that the subject be illuminated from the front and side, or from the side only, so that the light *models* the object, emphasizing its shape through value, tone, light, and shadow (fig. 237).

The first stage

241

242

243

I first draw the subject in charcoal, emphasizing the shadow of the bottle and the fruit, but not that of the background. Then I spray the drawing with a fixative. I begin to paint by staining the largest areas of the surface—the background—in order to avoid false contrasts (fig. 240). I continue by painting the local and projected shadows cast by the fruit, then the fold of the tablecloth in the foreground and the colors of the bottle (figs. 241 and 242). I then move quickly on to the fruit, and thus reach the end of this first stage (fig. 243).

Notice that I have not yet painted the foreground, which is the tablecloth covering the table. This is because the tablecloth is white (the same as the canvas, of course), which cannot produce false contrasts (refer to fig. 176 and 177 on page 71). I will paint it now, however.

Figs. 241 to 243. I paint the shadows first, then add the colors of the objects in order to complete the first stage.

Value painting

After painting the tablecloth, I then move on to the other orange, the white fruit bowl, and the yellow apple in the foreground (figs. 244 and 245). To emphasize the shape of the apple I create a *provoked contrast*, which is a false line or shadow (fig. 246). As you can see in the photograph on page 98 (fig. 237), this line or shadow does not really exist.

I paint the apple in the fruit bowl, blending with my fingers, a common technique among many artists (fig. 247); then I work on the final details. As shown in figures 248 and 249, I then paint a dark line to highlight the orange in the distance in order to dis-

tinguish it from the background. To do this, I first paint the line with a no. 4 sable brush, without worrying too much about "overstepping the line" on the outer edge (fig. 249). Then I thin out and mark it with a thicker brush using the light gray of the background. This marking almost erases the first line, as you can see in the finished painting (fig. 250). But there it is, successfully separating the orange from the background.

Figs. 244 to 247. I paint using a rapid technique. I follow the rule "what's done, is done," so that the two oranges, the apples, and the bananas and the red apple in the white bowl are practically the same as they appear in the finished painting (on the opposite page). There is still some touching up to do, however: the tablecloth's shadow, the area to the right of the orange in the foreground, and the gray line next to the yellow apple (fig. 246). The last two details were both designed to emphasize the shape and color of the fruit.

244

245

246

247

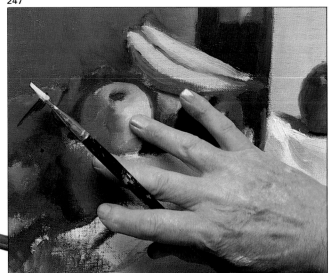

The second stage

248

249

Figs. 248 to 250. Still using a rapid technique, I paint a line to highlight the orange in the background and do the same with the apple. I have reduced the size of the shadow of the orange to make it look more natural and painted the shadow of the fold in the tablecloth in the foreground, but aside from that very little else, as you can see in the finished painting (fig. 250). An unexceptional painting, but one that distinctly shows the value style of painting.

Look at the orange in the foreground in the finished painting, and you will see that I painted a false, gray shadow that is almost completely invisible yet still produces the desired effect. Notice the finishing touches: the folds and the shadow of the tablecloth in the foreground, the bottle, the red cloth, the red reflection on the fruit bowl, the beets, then the background.

When we consider the final painting, I must stress that the term "value painting" does not refer to a particular style, but is rather a standard, classical approach to painting. The aim of this first exercise is to emphasize the fundamental differences between as the *two* approaches, of *value* and of *color*, and to try apply an understanding of these differences our painting, as we will do on the next page.

250

Colorist painting

251

252

253

254

As you know, *colorism* was introduced to the public for the first time in an exhibition organized by the *fauves* in Paris in 1906.

Apart from choosing a predominantly colorful model, frontal lighting is recommended so as to eliminate shadows and highlight colors. But the basic feature of colorist painting is the *interpretation*, the ability to imagine and see the necessary changes to express to the subject: what to remove, reduce, replace, add, move; in short, to paint in a *colorist* style.

Using a *colorist* interpretation of the same model (refer to fig. 237), I have eliminated the shadows by painting flat colors; replaced the dark background with a light one, adding a bluish-gray plane that extends behind the bottle (modifying its shape), and have moved the dark, blue plane toward the left. I have omitted the tablecloth and imagined another perspective, and used different shapes and colors on the table.

Notice that the first step in *colorist* painting is to compose the subject, not with charcoal and by drawing shadows as we did before, but by using paint, brush, and heavy lines to shape the objects (fig. 251).

Figs. 251 to 253. Although the objects are the same, they are composed differently to enhance the colorist approach. Once again, the shapes of the objects are sketched in, though this time without shadows. The sketch is less precise in this case, drawn with brush and oil paint, in ultramarine blue and umber. Next, as before, filling spaces, but with a colorist's eye.

Fig. 254. Vivid and flat, shadowless colors. Notice how, imitating the style of the *fauvists*, I try to maintain the original lines that shape the fruit, the bottle, the beets, and so on.

Figs. 255 to 257. Whether using brushes or fingers, it is essential to paint with clean pigments, never forgetting that the painting must be a spectacle of light. Brushes must be kept clean (fig. 257) in order to obtain consistently clean, vivid colors.

255

256

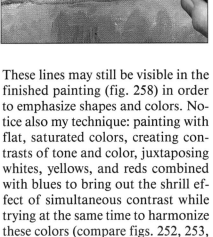

257

These lines may still be visible in the finished painting (fig. 258) in order to emphasize shapes and colors. Notice also my technique: painting with flat, saturated colors, creating contrasts of tone and color, juxtaposing whites, yellows, and reds combined with blues to bring out the shrill effect of simultaneous contrast while trying at the same time to harmonize these colors (compare figs. 252, 253, 254, and 256 with the finished painting, fig. 258).

Finally, let me remind you about the importance of working with clean brushes. Particularly when changing from dark to light tones, squeeze brushes between some pieces of newspaper and old rags and clean them with turpentine if necessary (fig. 257).

258

Fig. 258. The finished *colorist* painting. It is a question of imagining the colors, partially ignoring the subject itself while putting an emphasis on its shapes and colors. In this way it is possible to remove, replace, emphasize, change—in other words, to *interpret*, which is the fundamental aim of colorist painting.

The artist and the manufacture of colors

In Leonardo's and Michelangelo's time (from the second half of fifteenth century to the mid-sixteenth century), the artist was considered a craftsman. Both Leonardo and Michelangelo, privileged artists of their time, fought for social recognition. History tells us that on one occasion, when Michelangelo requested an audience with Pope Julius II and the servants in the antechamber refused him access, the artist felt he had been scorned and left Rome for Florence that same day, despite the Pope's pleas. He would return to Rome thirty years later.

In 1598, Cardinal Montalto, legate of the Pope, granted the founding of the first painters guild. However, the traditional system of training used in the artist's workshops remained unchanged. In his book *Academies of Art*, professor Nikolaus Pevsner explains the training of a fifteenth-century artist: "At the age of twelve or older, a boy could enter a workshop as an apprentice, and in two to six years could learn everything he needed: from grinding the colors to preparing backgrounds for drawing (dyeing the drawing paper) and canvas backgrounds (priming). After finishing his apprenticeship he could become an assistant, and after several more years he could obtain his certificate as master of the local guild, entitling him to set up as an independent painter.''

Figs. 259 and 260. The first solid tablet of watercolor paint (fig. 259) and the development of oil paints packaging. Skin pouches were first used, then glass containers, which evolved into today's tubes.

Fig. 261. Juan José Horemanns, *The Painter's Workshop*. Private collection, Madrid. At right the painter's apprentice grinds his master's colors.

259

260

261

The apprenticeship system was so strict that, according to Pevsner, the painters guild of Genoa denounced the nobleman Giovanni Battista "with burning hatred" because he had acquired a reputation as a self-taught painter, without having served a master as an apprentice.

What was involved in the job of "grinding the colors"? Cennino Cennini said that "the apprentice, in the fourteenth and fifteenth centuries, spent six years grinding colors, cooking the glue, and kneading the plaster." All the ancient books and documents that refer to the masters' workshops describe a large room with an adjoining rudimentary laboratory where the apprentice, under the master's guidance, would grind the pigments, create the oil and tempera vehicles, and prepare the solutions, primers, and other chemicals.

Figure 261 reproduces the painting by Juan José Horemanns, *The Painter's Workshop*, where you can see the artist talking to clients as they observe the artist working. On the right you can see the apprentice grinding colors. At his worktable there are some bowls and flasks that presumably contained the solutions for dissolving and mixing powdered pigment. Until the seventeenth century, the painter's palette was the tabletop where the artist would mix the colors, filling flasks and containers with the prepared color. In the early nineteenth century, oil colors were first manufactured and sold in small skin pouches that were stoppered with thumbtacks (fig. 260). In 1832, the Englishman William Winsor began to sell watercolors in small tin containers (fig. 259); in 1840, with Henry Charles Newton, he introduced the first oil paints in glass containers, which eventually evolved into today's tin tube.

The quality of the major brands of oil paints, watercolors, pastels, and other colors (figs. 262 to 264) ensure the finest results when creating a work of art.

Figs. 262 to 264. Modern manufacturing techniques of oil paints. Courtesy of Talens.

262

263

264

The composition and characteristics of pigments and colors

Now we are going to discuss the most commonly used colors or pigments for oil painting, watercolor painting, pastels, tempera, and other media. Keep in mind that colors begin as powdered pigments that, after being ground and bound with fatty oils and esthers, resins, balsams, and waxes, are transformed into oil paints, and when mixed or bound with water, gum arabic, honey, and glycerine, become watercolor paints. Powdered pigments can be grouped into major categories: *whites, yellows, browns, blacks, siennas and reds, and greens and blues*.

WHITES
Lead or silver white. Consists of white lead mixed with a small amount of zinc oxide. It has extraordinary covering power, dries quickly, and is very useful for applying as a thick paste for backgrounds and early painting stages. It is poisonous, and is not used to make watercolor paints.

Zinc white. Consists of zinc oxide crushed in poppy oil. Zinc white is whiter than lead white but covers less well, dries more slowly, and has a tendency to crack.

Titanium white (fig. 265). Basically composed of titanium oxide and heavy white. This is a modern pigment with great covering power, opacity, and drying speed; it is highly regarded by most artists.

China white. A thicker variety of zinc white, this is a special watercolor pigment. Zinc white is also sometimes sold as China white, so check its opacity on a piece of black paper. According to watercolor purists, white is not a color; only the white of the paper should be used.

YELLOWS
Naples yellow. In watercolor, consists of cadmium sulfide, ferrous oxide, and zinc oxide; in oils, consists of lead white, cadmium yellow, yellow ocher, and red brown. Both forms are poisonous. Rubens used this color, which dates back to the fifth century B.C., to paint flesh tones.

Cadmium lemon yellow (fig. 266). Made from cadmium sulfite. Considered to be one of the three primary pigment colors, it is a good, strong, brilliant color, though rather slow drying.

Cadmium yellow medium (fig. 267). Made from cadmium sulfite, which is used to make a range of yellows, from lemon yellow to orange yellow. Discovered in 1817, cadmium yellows are starting to replace chrome yellows.

Chrome yellow. Made with lead chromate and therefore poisonous, this pigment is available in several hues, ranging from very pale to almost orange. It is opaque and dries well, but tends to darken over time.

265 266 267 268

Yellow ocher (fig. 268). Made from natural earth containing hydrous ferric oxide, this basic color has been in use since prehistoric times. It has great covering power and permanence, and mixes easily with any other color.

BROWNS

Raw umber and burnt umber (figs. 269 and 270). The former is composed of raw umber with ferric oxides and manganese dioxide. Both are very dark colors, though raw umber has a slightly greenish tinge to it and burnt umber tends toward red. Both colors can be used in all techniques but will eventually blacken over time. They dry very quickly, so avoid applying them in thick layers to prevent cracking.

Vay Dyke brown (fig. 271). Essentially raw umber containing ferric oxide. This brown has a dark tone similar to that of the umbers, but tends toward a dark gray or almost black. It can be used for glazing, retouching, and covering small areas, and is more suited to watercolor than to oil. It is not recommended for painting in fresco.

BLACKS

Lamp black. A traditional color, it is a velvety powder, a variety of charcoal black obtained from burning hydrocarbons using a special procedure. A cold black, it can be used in all techniques.

Ivory black (fig. 272). A color obtained from burning animal bones, used equally in oil and watercolor. Mixed with cadmium yellow, it produces an extraordinary range of greens. Ivory black is a warm shade, deeper than lamp black. It can be used in all painting techniques.

Figs. 265 to 272. Despite the technological sophistication of the printing process, reproducing a specific color on paper is a difficult task. We must remember that the colors you see here have been printed using only four colors (the same as our primary pigment colors): yellow, cyan blue, and magenta with black. So it is not surprising that the *cadmium lemon yellow* on the opposite page (fig. 266) is not as bright as the actual pigment, and that the *cadmium yellow medium* (fig. 267) is so intense that it appears identical to *cadmium dark*. We are sometimes pleasantly surprised to see that hues as subtle as the cool *raw umber* or the warm *burnt umber* have been reproduced perfectly. You should always check the name of each color against the actual color in the tube of paint.

269 270 271 272

The composition and characteristics of pigments and colors

SIENNAS AND REDS

Raw sienna (fig. 273). As is yellow ocher, raw sienna is made from natural earth containing iron and manganese, which in its natural state is a rich, dark ocher color. It is a stable pigment except when diluted in a large quantity of oil, in which case there a risk of blackening exists.

Burnt sienna (fig. 274). Similar to raw sienna in makeup but containing a larger proportion of manganese, burnt sienna is a warmer, deeper color with a reddish tendency. It was widely used by the old masters, mainly the Venetians, and certain authors maintain that it was used by Rubens for painting his brilliant red flesh colors and their reflections. A stable color that can be used without limitations.

Cadmium red (fig. 275). Contains cadmium sulfite and selenic cadmi-um. Cadmium red can be dark or light; it is a clean color, with strong coloring power. A preferable substitute for vermilion which, in addition to its slow drying time and tendency to blacken when exposed to sunlight, is poisonous. Cadmium red was first introduced in Germany in 1907 and has been used throughout Europe since 1912.

Alizarin crimson (fig. 276). Alizarin crimson mixed with white becomes *magenta*, which, as you know, is one of the three primary pigment colors. It is composed of a lake that is 1:2 dihydroxyanthraquinone. Composed at that time of the root of *Rubia tinctorum*, it was used in ancient Egypt, Greece, and Rome. It was abandoned during the Renaissance but came back into fashion during the eighteenth and nineteenth centuries. Winsor & Newton admit in one of their publications that modern alizarin crimson "does not possess the beauty of the lakes obtained from the root of the plant."

GREENS AND BLUES

Permanent green. A mixture of emerald green and cadmium lemon yellow, permanent green is a luminous green, either pale or deep. It is a stable color without limitations.

Figs. 273 to 280. Again we see small errors when reproducing certain colors. The *burnt sienna* is more reddish, the *cadmium red* is much redder, and on the next page, the *ultramarine blue deep* should be a little more violet and the *Prussian blue* should contain a slight leaning toward green. Study these pigment names against actual samples of oil paints.

273 274 275 276

Earth green (fig. 277). Made of "king's silver" or copper acetoarsenite. Known also as *viridian green*, it should not be confused with *opaque green*. On certain color charts it is also referred to as "emerald green," which has many disadvantages and limitations. Earth green is considered the best green for its covering capacity, richness, stability, and safety.

Cobalt blue (fig. 278). Contains cobalt aluminate or cobalt phosphate with some alumina. Available in light and dark shades, it can be used in all painting techniques without limitations. This blue covers well and dries relatively easily, though when used in oils it may acquire a slightly greenish cast over time.

Ultramarine blue deep (fig. 279). Pure ultramarine blue, ground from the semiprecious stone lapis lazuli, is the most expensive of all pigments, worth over twice its weight in gold. One of the largest deposits of lapis lazuli is located in Kikcha, Afghanistan. Used in Europe since the twelfth century, in 1828 a Frenchman named Guimet discovered artificial ultramarine blue, which he obtained by mixing aluminum, silica, soda, and sulfate. The quality and affordability of artificial ultramarine blue have made it an excellent substitute for the legendary original pigment.

Prussian blue (fig. 280). Composed of potassium ferricyanide, it is a powerful, transparent, quick-drying color with the sole disadvantage of fading slightly when exposed to light. Prussian blue mixed with white takes on the same hue as *cyan blue*, one of the three primary pigment colors. It is also sometimes called *Paris blue* and is offered by some manufacturers under their own trade names (for example, Rembrandt blue), as is also the case with earth green.

Phthalo blue. Made from copper phthalocyanine, this organic pigment was introduced in 1937 by Imperial Chemical Industries Ltd. With its great staining power, transparency, and safety, some artists prefer it to Prussian blue.

277   278   279   280

Colors: How many and which to use?

Some colors charts for both oils and watercolors offer an assortment of over two hundred colors; on one chart I counted over fifteen yellows: cadmium lemon yellow, cadmium yellow pale, chrome yellow pale, chrome lemon yellow, cadmium yellow, cadmium yellow dark, Indian yellow, Brilliant yellow light, Naples yellow light, Naples yellow dark, Naples yellow-red, and so on. There were twenty-one oranges, reds, and crimsons; thirty-six blues and greens....

Of course, nobody uses this many colors; besides, everyone wants to use *their own* colors, *their own* palette. So there are artists who use cerulean blue (similar to cyan blue) instead of cobalt blue; and those who add cadmium orange, chrome yellow, or sap green "in order to break up the green hues," or cobalt green to "create transparencies."

On one point, however, all artists agree: the number of colors. For oil painting, there is a maximum of twelve (plus black and white); for watercolor painting, the palette boxes restrict the number of paints. The largest watercolor palettes have twenty-four containers (for twenty-three colors plus black), but it's not really necessary to use them all. This is proven by the fact that the palette boxes that come with tubes of creamy watercolor, the most common among professional watercolor painters, contain only twelve colors.

The English watercolor masters of the eighteenth century, such as Girtin, Cox, Cozens, and even the great Turner, painted with no more than five or six colors. Cennini had already advocated the use of a limited number of colors in oil painting. Titian always worked with a very limited range of colors and stated: "One can be a great painter using only three colors." In his analysis of the colors used by the Renaissance artists, scholar, author, and renowned

French painter Maurice Bousset stated that "with only five colors (two blues, lapis lazuli and German blue; two reds, red ocher and madder lake; and one yellow, yellow ocher) with added *verdaccio*, they were able to obtain their most vivid harmonies of color." And when ascertaining the number of colors commonly used by present-day artists, Bousset himself states that "most of the great impressionists used no more than six colors" and suggests a list of ten colors, including black and white. I agree with his choices entirely, but would add, however, four more, three of which are optional. See for yourself the assortment of colors I propose for oil and watercolor painting in the boxes and in figures 281 and 282 on the opposite page. For watercolors I have included an additional color, *Payne's gray*, commonly found on the watercolorist's palette.

What I have said so far holds true for watercolor painting, oil painting, acrylics, gouache, and tempera; these media require only ten or twelve colors to paint all the colors in nature. But this does not apply to pastels. As you know, in watercolor painting, and especially in oils, in order to paint, for example, a certain flesh color, you may need to mix white, yellow, ocher, blue, and crimson. These mixtures are rather complex in pastel painting; it is always preferable to work directly with the specific color, be it lighter, darker, or with a reddish, blue, green, or pink tendency. This is why pastels or come in such vast assortments—up to 300, and even 528 colors (as you saw on page 35).

COLORS COMMONLY USED IN OIL PAINTING

*1. Cadmium lemon yellow
2. Cadmium yellow medium
3. Yellow ocher
*4. Burnt sienna
5. Burnt umber
6. Light vermilion
7. Deep madder
*8. Permanent green
9. Emerald green
10. Cobalt blue deep
11. Ultramarine blue deep
12. Prussian blue
Titanium white
*Ivory black

If you wish to reduce this list, you can exclude the three colors that are marked with an asterisk and black.

COLORS COMMONLY USED IN WATERCOLOR PAINTING

1. Lemon yellow
2. Dark yellow
3. Yellow ocher
4. Umber
5. Sepia
6. Cadmium red
7. Madder
8. Permanent green
9. Emerald green
10. Cobalt blue
11. Ultramarine blue
12. Prussian blue
13. Payne's gray
Ivory black

Figs. 281 to 283. Oil and watercolor pigments commonly used by professional artists. Except for the addition of *Payne's gray* and the absence of *white* on the list of watercolors they are basically the same. The assortment of pastel colors shows only a small sample of the pigments available.

281

282

283

In a book about color an *overview of color mixes* is essential, since it will help to determine differences among and tendencies of similar colors and the various ranges possible when mixing them with others. We will also look at the influence of certain colors due to their dyeing capacity, and analyze mixes of complementary colors and the composition of neutral colors. We will also see how it is not merely by coincidence that paintings are dominated by certain colors. It is all a question of the use of *color ranges*, which are composed of a series of harmonized colors. In this chapter we will analyze the three basic color ranges: *warm*, *cool*, and *neutral* colors.

COLOR MIXES AND RANGES

A study of color mixes

285 **Lemon yellow**

286 **Cadmium yellow medium**

287 **Yellow ocher**

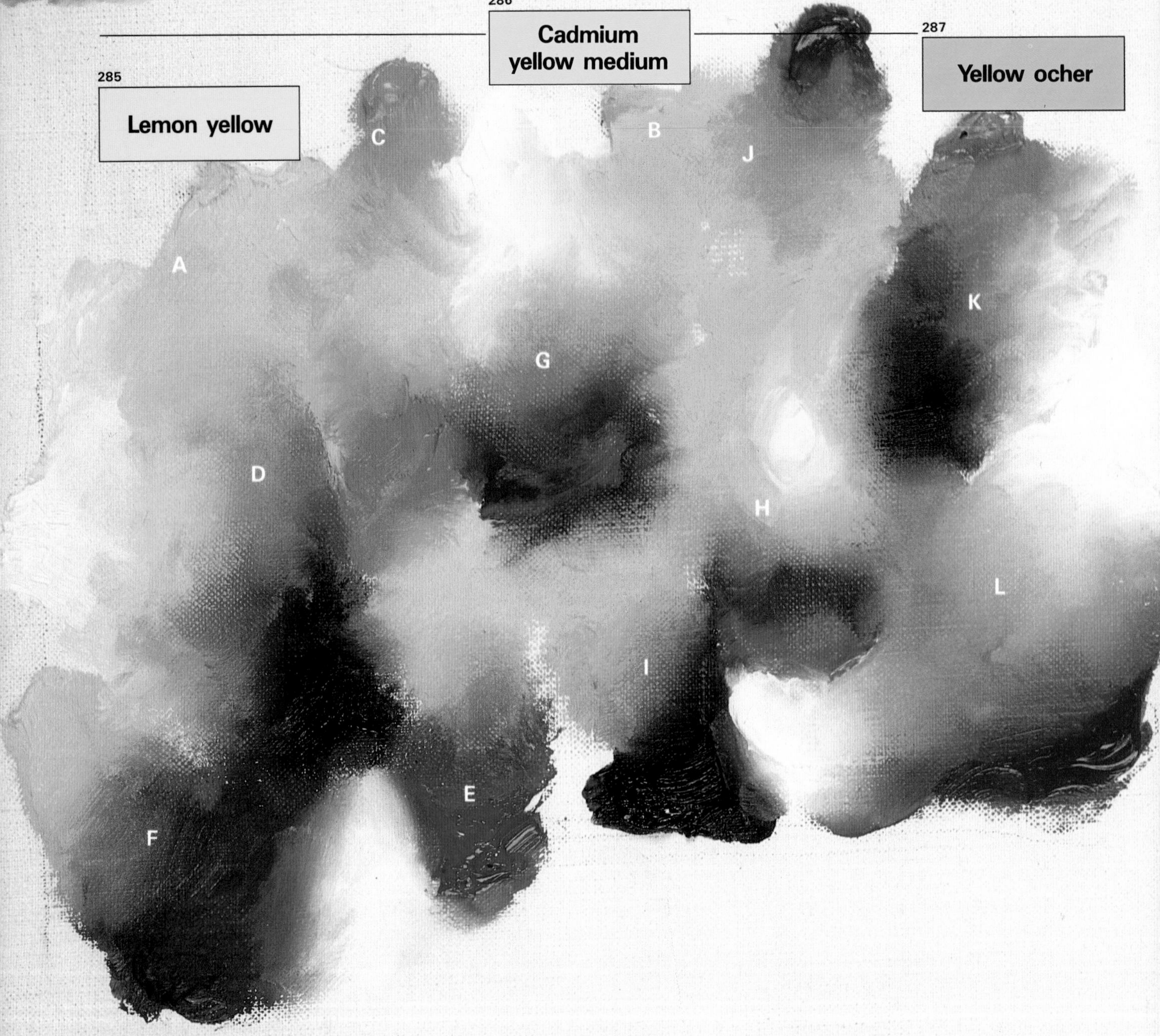

Yellows and ochers mixed with blue, vermilion, and carmine

Note how the two yellows differ: lemon yellow (A) and cadmium yellow medium (B). Lemon yellow is lighter and tends toward green, even when mixed with white. When mixed with vermilion, ocher, and white (C), it gives off a bright range of flesh colors. Combined with Prussian blue we get the bright green that you can see in (D), which dirties a little when mixed with cobalt blue (E), and even more so with ultramarine blue (F).

Cadmium yellow medium is darker, verging on orange (B), which becomes a creamy yellow when mixed with white. The mix of this yellow with ultramarine blue results in a dirty, neutral green (G), which becomes a brownish black when mixed in equal parts, due to the fact the two are complementaries. This creamy yellow can become olive green when combined with cobalt blue (H) and Prussian blue (I). When mixed with carmine, cadmium yellow medium changes to a chromatically rich dark orange (J).

Mixing yellow ocher with ultramarine blue results in a dirty, neutral green (K), and when combined with white, carmine, deep madder, and ultramarine blue, we get a darker range of flesh colors (L).

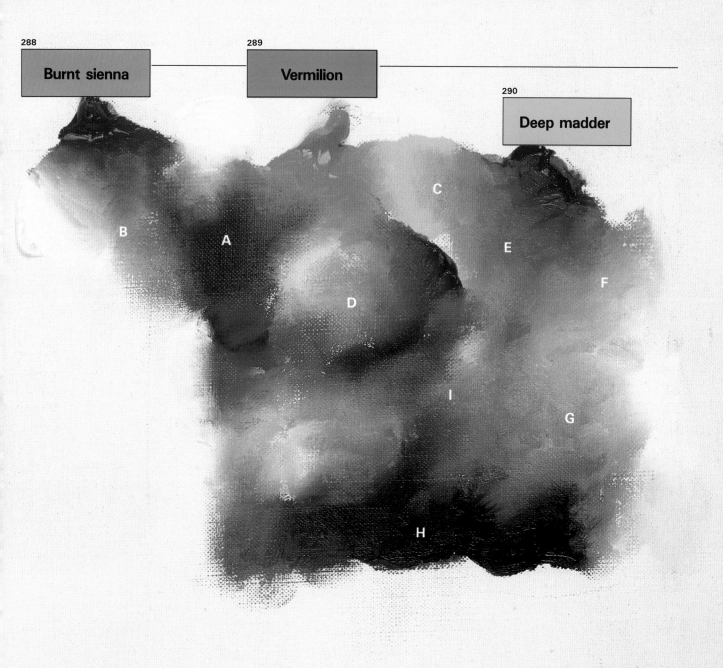

288 Burnt sienna

289 Vermilion

290 Deep madder

Burnt sienna, vermilion, and carmine mixed with yellow, blue, and green
When mixed with ultramarine blue, both burnt sienna and vermilion produce black (A); by then adding white, a range of neutral grays appears (B). Vermilion and yellow together make orange, which darkens when mixed with carmine (C). Carmine mixed with ultramarine blue produces purple and violet. Observe in (E) the dyeing capacity of deep madder which, when mixed with white, becomes magenta—a primary

pigment color (F). When combining magenta with emerald green and white, we get grayish hues of a greenish or carmine tendency (G). Because they are complementary colors, deep madder and emerald green together make black (H). See also how this mix of green, carmine, and blue produces neutral tones when mixed with yellow (I).

Figs. 285 to 287. A study of color mixes: yellows and ochers with blue, vermilion, and carmine.

Figs. 288 to 290. Burnt sienna, vermilion, and carmine mixed with yellow, blue, and green.

A study of color mixes

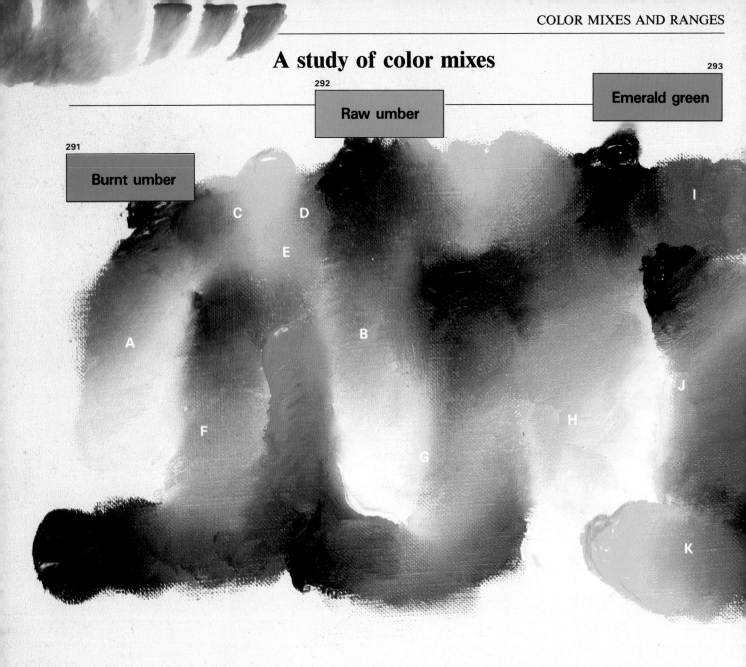

291 **Burnt umber**

292 **Raw umber**

293 **Emerald green**

Burnt umber and raw umber mixed with white, Prussian blue, yellow, and vermilion

Are earth colors black? No. They look black, but they are actually very dark brown. At first glance they look the same, but when mixed with white burnt umber has a slighly warm, reddish tendency (A), while raw umber—a cooler, more neutral color—is almost a dark or blackish gray (B). These slight differences are important, especially when both colors are mixed with yellow (C and D): burnt umber mixed with lemon

yellow is greener (E). There are also notable differences in tone when both umbers are mixed with blue and white (F and G), especially when you take into account that the shadows of many light objects must be resolved with white, blue, and a little raw or burnt umber, depending on whether the shadow is warm or cool.

Emerald green mixed with white, ocher, blue, and yellow

Note the wide range of colors that emerald can produce when mixed with white (H) and other colors. This

powerful dyeing color is striking and flashy, and a little overpowering when used alone. However, it is excellent for mixing. When combined with ocher (I), we get warm neutral greens; mixed with ultramarine blue (J), it procedures a magnificent contrast; with yellow (K), we obtain the brightest of all greens.

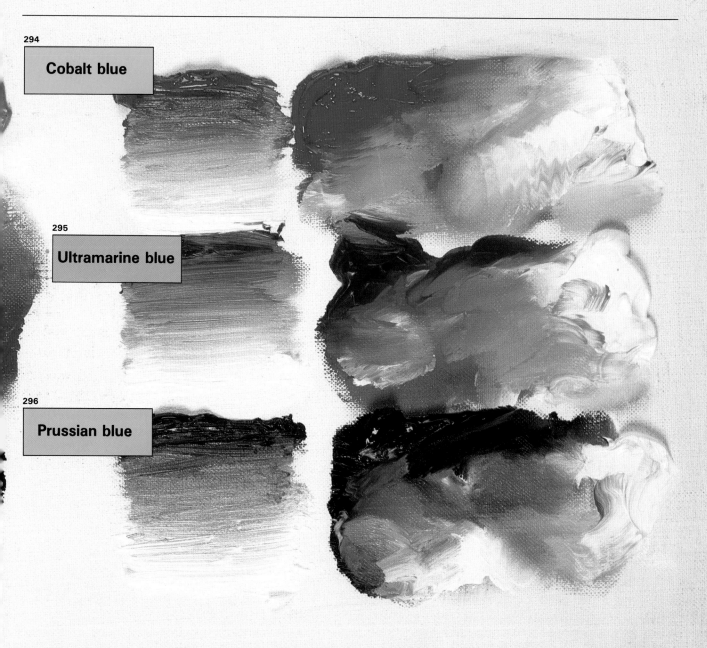

294 Cobalt blue

295 Ultramarine blue

296 Prussian blue

Three blues: cobalt, ultramarine, and Prussian blue

It is difficult to determine the differences among various blues, but knowing what these differences are is and fundamental for resolving colors and mixes. With these three blues it is possible to make countless distinct tones when mixed with white. We could define *cobalt blue* as a neutral blue, a "blue blue," which makes colors in shadow appear brighter and more transparent. *Ultramarine blue* contains a heavy carmine influence. This makes it very convenient to use

in opaque, dark, or dirty shadow. *Prussian blue* is a very intense and radiant blue, capable of obliterating any color near it. On the other hand, when used in small quantities it produces extraordinary transparent hues. When combined with white, it tends toward gray and illuminates any color.

Figs. 291 to 293. Burnt and raw umber mixed with white, Prussian blue, yellow, and vermilion.

Figs. 294 to 296. A study of three blues: cobalt, ultramarine, and Prussian.

Harmonizing colors

In 1649, King Philip IV of Spain sent Velázquez on his second trip to Rome to buy paintings. Velázquez was received with great honor, although not as an artist but as one of the king's closest friends. He was so irritated by this that only a few days after his arrival he painted a portrait of his servant, Juan de Pareja, then ordered him to show it to several Roman aristocrats and artists so that they could see both the model and his painting.

Juan de Pareja (fig. 297) and his portrait of Pope Innocent X (painted a year later) are two of Velázquez's most celebrated portraits. This is due to two basic factors: first, Velázquez's "rapid stroke," referred to at that time as "painting in blotches" or "painting with separate stains," which we would now call the *impressionist way of painting*. The other reason is his color range, which Ortega y Gasset called a "low palette" because it is composed of "dark and olive greens, opaque whites and blacks." This range also contained ochers, browns, grays, and blacks, which together compose a *succession of perfectly harmonized colors*, or a *determined color range*.

A painting can certainly be based on a series of grayish and brownish tones and colors, and Velázquez's works are an example of this (fig. 298). In that case a *neutral color range* was used. When we paint with colors that tend toward red, we are using a *warm range of colors*. If the colors have a bluish tendency, then we are using a *cool range of colors*. We will study these ranges in more detail a little later in this section. Color ranges can usually be observed in the subject itself, thanks to a natural tendency for colors to relate. This tendency is sometimes very strong; for instance, at dawn on a cloudy day, when grays and blues predominate, or at sunset, when everything looks gold, yellow, and red. However, color harmony in nature is not always so evident, so the artist must organize, accentuate, and even exaggerate a determined color range, obsessively following it, as he or she creates the picture.

297

Figs. 297 and 298. Velázquez, *Juan de Pareja* and *Garden at the Villa Médici*. The Prado, Madrid. Most of Velázquez's works were painted with browns, grays, dirty ochers, dark greens, olives, opaque whites, and blacks, all of which make up the *neutral range of colors*.

298

Figs. 299 to 301. José M. Parramón, *Flowers, Path through the Wood*, and *Notre Dame*. These three pictures use the three different ranges: warm, cool, and neutral, respectively.

299

300

301

The harmonic range of two colors and white

302

As you can see in figure 303, it is perfectly possible to paint an oil painting with just two colors and white, or to paint a watercolor with just these two colors (remember that in watercolor painting the color white is the white of the paper).

To paint the still life in oils shown opposite, I used *titanium white, English red light*, and *ultramarine blue*. You should choose a subject whose tones can be reproduced from the two colors you might choose, which should be complementary in order to produce black when mixed together, and to obtain a wide range of tones when mixed with white. In the previous example you can see the range of bluish grays in the drape in the background on the left, in the bottle, in the neutral gray with reddish tendencies in the right-hand part of the background, and in the shadowed portion of the white ceramic jug. I used English red light to paint the wine and the apple, and for the ceramic jug's decoration and the grapes I used ultramarine blue. Naturally, using just two colors has some limitations. For instance, the color of the apple was really carmine with orange tones in its lit areas, but as you can see in figure 302 the number of possible ranges and colors obtained by mixing dark ultramarine blue, English red, and white is quite ample.

Taking into account the subject's tones, other possible color combinations are:

carmine, emerald green, and white
burnt umber, Prussian blue, and white
Indian red, permanent green deep, and white

I have said it before many times but I will say it again: Practice painting with two colors. Besides helping you to acquire experience with a brush, it enables you to get to know the paint—its consistency, its covering power with or without turpentine, its drying time, and other details. If you are an art teacher, I recommend that you assign this exercise to your students.

Fig. 302. Sample palette obtained with two colors, English red light and ultramarine blue, plus white.

303

304

Figs. 303 and 304. I painted this still life with only two colors plus white. Few people would believe that it is possible to get so many colors and shades from only two colors. You can achieve the same results using the very same colors with little difficulty.

The harmonic range of warm colors

305

The painting in figure 307 is basically composed of yellows, ochers, oranges, reds, and carmines. Theoretically, the range of warm colors includes only those shown in the box below (fig. 306). But in practice, if we think about the colors that are near to red and yellow on the spectrum and look back at page 111 (fig. 281), we can select the following colors to make up the range of warm colors:

Lemon yellow, cadmium yellow, ocher, burnt sienna, burnt umber, vermilion, madder lake, permanent green, emerald green, ultramarine blue, and black.

Ultramarine blue possesses a reddish tendency, but this does not mean that cobalt blue or Prussian blue cannot be included in a range of warm colors. The sample range on this page is a good example of this (fig. 305).

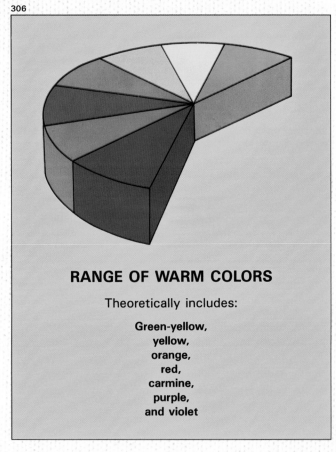

306

RANGE OF WARM COLORS

Theoretically includes:

**Green-yellow,
yellow,
orange,
red,
carmine,
purple,
and violet**

Figs. 305 to 307. José M. Parramón, *Urban Landscape in a Village*. Private collection. Here is a good example of the range of warm colors combined with one or two neutral and cool colors.

307

The harmonic range of cool colors

308

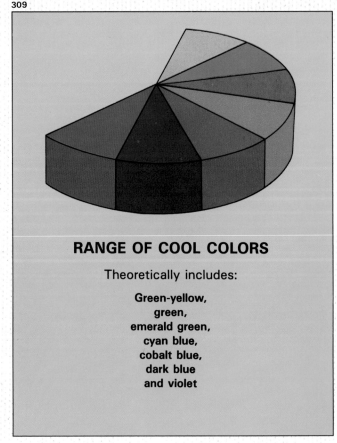

309

Although the range of cool colors is basically blue in tendency, it can easily harmonize with greens, violets, carmines, grays, browns, blacks, and, on certain occasions, with reds, yellows, ochers, and siennas. Refer to Mary Cassatt's painting (fig. 171) where a child depicted in warm color sits in the center of a blue interior. Look also at *Entering the Village* on the opposite page (fig. 310); blue predominates, but there is contrast of warm color in the center of the subject.

As we said before, the range of cool colors is theoretically made up of those included in the adjoining box (fig. 309). But in practice the colors that artists use in this range are:

Prussian blue, ultramarine blue, cobalt green, emerald green, permanent green, madder lake, burnt umber, ocher, and yellow.

As a complement to this instruction, study the sample palette at the top of pages 124 and 125 (fig. 308).

RANGE OF COOL COLORS

Theoretically includes:

Green-yellow,
green,
emerald green,
cyan blue,
cobalt blue,
dark blue
and violet

Figs. 308 to 310. José M. Parramón, *Entering the Village*. The range of cool colors that I painted above it inspired this study, which is a good example of their use in a composition.

310

The harmonic range of neutral colors

If you mix two complementaries together in equal parts, you get black. If you then add white you get a more or less neutral gray, depending on the amount of white you add. But if you take two complementary colors—for example, ultramarine blue and lemon yellow—and you mix them together in *unequal parts* and add white, you get a dirty green-gray, which will tend toward either blue or yellow, depending on the proportions of your mix, and will be lighter or darker depending on how much white you use.

This is the theoretical formula for mixing a neutral color. However, in reality it is more intuitive: We paint what the model "tells" us to paint.

The landscape on the opposite page (fig. 313) is painted in a range of neutral, dirty, and gray colors, which is dictated by the model. Mix your colors to create a selection of neutral colors similar to the one at the top of this page (fig. 311).

Fig. 311. The range of neutral colors that was used in the painting opposite.

Fig. 313. José M. Parramón, *Rupit Landscape*. Private collection. All the colors in this landscape have a grayish, broken tendency.

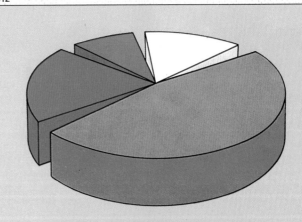

RANGE OF NEUTRAL COLORS

Theoretically comprised

of a mix of two complementary

colors in unequal

parts with white.

Within a range of broken colors we may find a tendency toward warm or cold tones, depending on the shades which predominate in the general color scheme of the painting. Warm tones may be used, such as reds, ochres, siennas, kakis, olive greens, and so on. On the other hand, the tonality could display a range of cold neutral colors: bluish, greenish, or violet shades, and so on.

313

In this section we present a sample of subjects and styles step-by-step, painted especially for this book, which sum up all of the technical and theoretical information discussed earlier. In an extraordinary collaboration of master painters, we present a selection of their pictures painted in oil, watercolor, and pastel.

COLOR AND PAINTING IN PRACTICE

314

Paintings by Badia Camps

Badia Camps is a famous *intimist* painter, which involves *painting figures in everyday scenes and domestic interiors*. Camps worked as an illustrator for European and American publishing houses until the end of the 1970s, when he decided to dedicate all of his time to painting. Since then he has held more than forty exhibitions in Europe and North and South America, and has received many important awards, including the Bastai Verlag Gold Medal of Germany and first prize from the Barcelona Chamber of Commerce. As you can see in these reproductions, Badia Camps paints pictures of exceptional quality. His carefully composed images prove him to be a master both of painting and drawing, with a special preference for ranges of warm neutral colors.

Figs. 315 to 320. A sampling of work by Badia Camps, an outstanding artist. He paints all types of subjects, but excels in figure paintings.

315

316

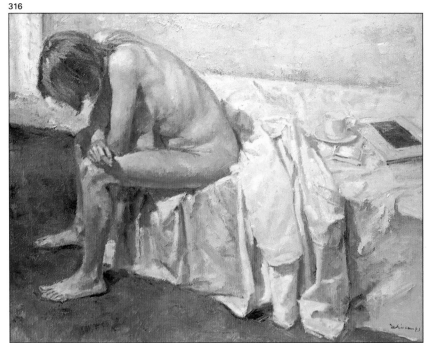

317

318

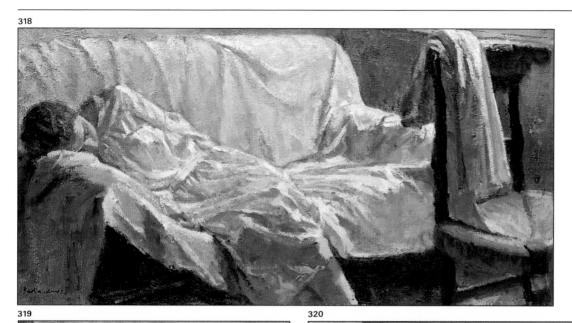

319

320

Camps paints a figure in a range of warm neutral colors

Badia always begins his paintings by doing a series of sketches or studies to determine how he will light the subject, pose the model, choose the elements that will accompany the model, resolve the point of view, and finalize the composition.

"Drawing is important," says Badia Camps as he shows me the sketches that are reproduced here on these pages. "It's necessary to draw every day, with a model and from nature. Draw and take notes of dressed figures and nudes every day, until you are totally familiar with the dimensions and proportions, as well as the anatomy and structure of the human body."

Look at the last of a series of sketches (fig. 321) and the painting for which the series was done (fig. 322). By seeing both at the same time, you will be able to compare and check the likeness of the pose and the composition, which Badia Camps obtains by framing the image in the sketch. On the opposite page you can see the first and last sketches in a series the artist drew for the picture he is about to paint for this book. In the first one, Camps has concentrated on the general composition (fig. 323). He has chosen a wide angle, placing the figure on the left and highlighting the rectangular shape of the table, which will probably accommodate a vase of flowers, a cup, and other small objects. The final and definitive sketch (fig. 324) shows a perfectly structured composition: The figure is leaning on a round table; she is resting or looking at some books. The angle of the composition, the point of view, and the lighting have all been finalized, so that Badia Camps may now begin his painting.

Figs. 321 and 322. Badia Camps never begins a painting without making an in-depth study of the setting, atmosphere, pose, point of view, and lighting, for which he makes several sketches, mostly in sepia-colored chalks and sometimes even in oils. Only once he is convinced that the basic factors have been resolved does he go on to paint the picture. Here we can see one of the sketches he made before beginning his painting (fig. 322).

321

322

Figs. 323 and 324. This is Badia Camps's first sketch, in which he has tried to express the initial idea: a woman sitting at a table. He has given great importance to the table within the lengthened format. "I believe the picture should adapt itself to the format and not the format to the picture. For that reason I never work with international canvas sizes," explains Badia Camps. In figure 324, the final sketch, the initial idea has evolved: The composition has been changed, although the figure is still the focus.

How Camps paints

Badia Camps begins his picture by drawing the subject on a white canvas using a brush with oil paints diluted in turpentine (fig. 325). Painting with cobalt blue, sienna, and white, he achieves a simple but accurate drawing that includes the forms, dimensions, and proportions of the painting he will soon begin. The artist applies what he calls a "bed of paint" onto the drawing. In reality, he is talking about an impasto of color that is resolved *au premier coup* (on the first attempt). With this first layer, he determines the painting's form, values, contrast, and color (fig. 326). In two or three sessions the artist will convert this sketch into the final painting.

325

326

Badia Camps will gradually perfect the color, lighting, contrast, and color harmony by superimposing thick impastos on top of other layers. "I normally paint three or four pictures at the same time," Badia Camps explains. "This gives me a chance to leave one aside to dry for a few days. Then I return to it and apply new color over the dry layer." The result of painting and repainting is clearly evident (fig. 327). The artist has successfully achieved a brighter atmosphere by replacing the warm colors with cooler ones: the ochers, siennas, and pinks are substituted with blues, grays, and yellow-

greens. He has also lightened and changed the color of the background in order to heighten the contrast (note the *frottage* of light on the blouse) and at the same time finalized the forms.

Fig. 325. Badia Camps begins his paintings by making the initial drawing with a brush and oil paints. For this he uses cobalt blue and sienna diluted with turpentine. As you can see, he has used very little paint for the sketch so that he can start painting immediately.

Fig. 326. The careful construction of the initial drawing (previous figure) enables Badia Camps to "fill" the picture in a maximum of one or two sessions. This also helps him to get a general idea of the contrast and color.

Fig. 327. It takes Badia Camps several sessions to finish the painting, during which he adjusts colors, hues, tendencies, and contrasts, and accentuates lights and shadows, taking advantage of the partially dry state of the painting. In the finished painting we can see the basic color changes that make the picture brighter and enhance the contrast.

327

Paintings by Vicenç Ballestar

Vicenç Ballestar is a versatile artist, capable of painting in oil, watercolor, pastel, crayons, colored pencils, and other media, although he is best known for his watercolors. Ballestar paints nudes, landscapes, seascapes, and still lifes; in fact, any subject under the sun. Not long ago, while visiting him at his studio, I came across a folder filled with notes and sketches of animals he had drawn at the zoo. Some had been done in pencil, some in pen, and one or two in watercolor. They were simply incredible; I was so impressed by them that I suggested that he edit a book called *How to Paint Animals* for the "Drawing and Painting" series. From then on I would see Ballestar practically every other day, which gave me the chance to get to know him as both a person and an artist. He is a great guy and a perfectionist in his work. Vicenç Ballestar is a good friend.

Figs. 328 to 333. Vicenç Ballestar is a watercolor master who has received countless awards and exhibited all over the world. But Ballestar also excels in oil, pastel, colored pencil, crayon, and oil pastel. The pictures illustrated on these pages—the nude, the two landscapes, and the seascape, all painted in watercolor; the cat, done in colored pencils; and the still life, painted in pastel—are just a few examples of this painter's incredible versatility.

328

329

330

331

332

333

Ballestar paints a landscape in watercolors using a range of neutral colors

334

Vicenç Ballestar is an original artist. He paints his watercolors on water-color paper mounted on interna-tional-sized stretchers, as if they were oil paintings. "You'll see," he says to me. "Before starting I soak the paper. Since it is mounted on a stretcher it is tensed perfectly. That avoids any fuss of mounting it with strips of tape." He draws his pictures with charcoal (fig. 334). "I use char-coal because it's not permanent; you can erase it with a damp cloth without dirtying the paper." One other thing: Ballestar is left-handed. Ballestar uses watercolor paints in tubes (mainly Rembrandt and Schmin-cker), and paints with a round No. 14 sable brush and three flat brush-es (a No. 10, a 2 cm, and a 2.5 cm).

336

Fig. 334. Ballestar resolves the initial drawing in charcoal by roughly sketching the subject and working out the basic foms. Then he erases most of the charcoal with a rag, leaving only a faint impression that enables him to paint without staining or dirtying his colors.

Fig. 335. Ballestar always paints from top to bottom so that he can definitively resolve specific areas of the picture.

335

338

337

Ballestar also uses Schoeller thick-grained watercolor paper, a metal palette with sixteen compartments, and a cloth for cleaning and drying his brushes (fig. 337).

Ballestar resolves the form and color at the same time; that is, *he paints and draws at the same time*, with the confidence and speed of an artist who has painted the same picture a thousand times (fig. 336). As if the brush had a life of its own, Ballestar runs it up and down the paper, outlining and reserving the white of the paper as he proceeds (fig. 335). Here we can see how the artist has painted the background of water with a dark neutral color (while reserving the white rocks) and then diluted it to get an almost imperceptible blue hue, with which he paints the foreground as a representation of the water's shimmering reflections. Ballestar then goes on to the grass where he applies a gold color (fig. 338). Finally, he paints the dark forms that are reflected on the water. And with that the first stage is finished (fig. 339).

But you must see the artist at work to understand Ballestar's capacity and ability. The zig-zag strokes that reproduce the reflections on the water were done with a 2-cm flat brush. The artist applied spontaneous, confident strokes and achieved the exact appearance of the water's reflections. And before that, he quickly went about drawing and painting, while at the same time reserving the trunks and branches in the tops of the two trees. But despite such extraordinary

talent, Ballestar is very humble: "Well," he says, "It's not that difficult. You know only too well that if I make a mistake, I can open up some of the whites and absorb the color with my brush."

Fig. 336. We can see Ballestar's method of resolving forms and colors from the very beginning. The top part of the picture is practically done; all that is left is to add one or two touches to intensify the contrast. Note how the artist has reserved whites in the trunks and branches in the tops of the trees.

Fig. 337. Ballestar uses a thick rag to dry and clean his brushes, something he does almost automatically.

Fig. 338. At this point, almost all the warm-colored grass has been resolved. He momentarily leaves the painting aside to let it dry.

Fig. 339. This is how Ballestar's painting looks at the end of the first stage, which required one hour and ten minutes to complete.

339

Second stage: technique and practice

340

Ballestar begins the second stage by resolving the colors and reflections of the water and finishing the rocks (fig. 340). Then he devotes time to details, absorbing color with his brush and opening up whites in the trunks and branches of the trees. See, for example, the area of small trunks in figure 341 before the whites were opened up. Note in figure 342 how Ballestar opens them to make thin branches by dampening them first and then absorbing the extra wetness with his brush. You can see the final results in figure 343 and figure 346 (the finished painting). Ballestar uses the same techniques in figures 344 and 345.

I ask Ballestar about the technical difficulties involved in watercolor. He answers: "If you think about it, the great masters of watercolor—Turner, Sorolla, Fortuny, Sargent, and Hopper—were also great oil painters. It's logical because oil painting entails no technical preoccupations. With watercolor you must *draw and paint* knowing that you've got to reserve this and outline that. It's something that very much preoccupies watercolorists without much experience."

"That's true," I say, "you're also a very good oil painter." Ballestar laughs and without looking up from his work says, "I didn't say it to flatter myself."

341

342

345

343

344

Figs. 341 to 345. Ballestar demonstrates here that thanks to the quality of the paper (Schoeller) he can open up the whites.

Fig. 340. Ballestar now adds the reflections to the water by applying zig-zag brushstrokes.

Fig. 346. The finished painting. Ballestar has proved once again his mastery of the medium.

346

Paintings by Juan Raset

Some years ago Juan Raset was a student of mine. Then he went on to work in technical drawing. He eventually gave it up because he was really devoted to oil painting, so he started again. After three or four exhibitions he changed to pastel painting, which he has been doing now since the mid-1980s. "I like playing with light and color," says Raset, "and pastel has the advantage of allowing you to get fast results. It's like watercolor: The critical moment is the first emotion, which affects whether it works." He specializes in female nudes and has exhibited in galleries on various occasions. As is immediately evident from his work, Juan Raset is an extraordinary pastelist.

Figs. 347 to 353. Here we have an excellent sampling of work by guest artist Juan Raset. Note the diversity in color harmony that his pictures provide. It is difficult to tell whether we should admire the confidence of his drawing or the richness and creativity of his use of color.

347

348

349

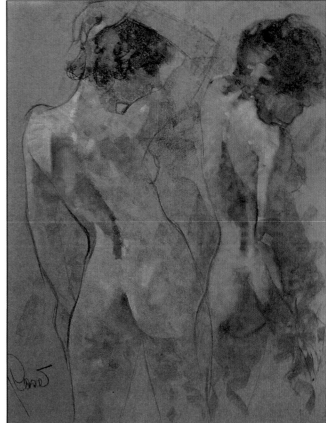

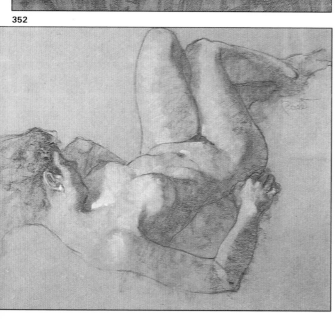

Raset paints a nude in pastel: "You draw as you paint"

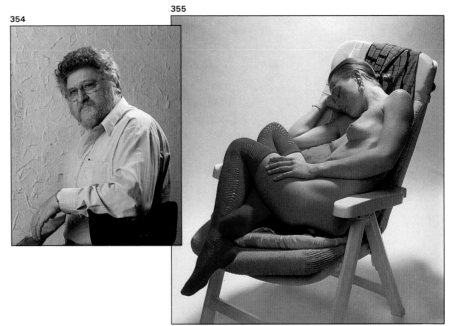

There are two ways to paint in pastel: One involves filling the whole paper, blending the color so that the finished work looks like an oil painting. That is how the famous pastelists of the eighteenth century (Rosalba Carriera, Quentin de Latour, Perronneau, and others) worked. The other pastel technique involves painting on colored paper, allowing the drawing and color of the paper to be seen, which is how most nineteenth-century artists worked, including Toulouse-Lautrec, Mary Cassatt, and the great master of pastel, Edgar Degas. Raset belongs to this second group: He draws and paints, paints and draws, as if he were determined to prove that it's possible to paint a drawing. But we will see what he does and how he does it. He is going to paint a female nude wearing red tights and sitting in a lounge chair. Behind her Raset has placed a blue towel (fig. 355).

Raset paints with Rembrandt pastel colors (soft), alternating them with Faber (slightly harder). He explains that the Faber pastels, due to their hardness, enable him to draw lines as thin as with pastel pencils, which he does not use (fig. 358). He uses a normal eraser, even though he says

Figs. 354, 355, and 358. Juan Raset, the posed model, and some of the colors that the artist will use (bottom left).

Figs. 356 and 357. First Raset sketches in graphite pencil, then erases most of it with a rag. Finally, he goes over the faint pencil lines with a dark chalk.

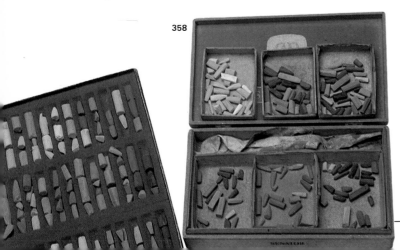

it is not good to erase, since it ruins the paper's fiber.

Raset outlines the model with an HB pencil on gray Canson Mi-Teintes paper (fig. 356). Once the initial drawing is finished, Raset removes the oil of the graphite by rubbing an old rag over the pencil marks.

The artist then reinstates the initial structure of the composition using a very sharp piece of sepia-colored chalk. He alternates these thin lines with wide strokes, checking for possible gradation of form and shadow (figs. 357 and 359).

Using dark red English chalk, Raset then proceeds to apply thick strokes by working with the chalk's flat side. In this way he marks out the parts in shadow and accentuates their borders. At this point, however, he is still only in the sketching phase (figs. 360 to 362).

Figs. 359 to 362. Raset dedicates the rest of this first stage to redrawing the nude with a piece of English red chalk, while at the same time putting in the first lights and shadows.

359

360

361

362

Raset paints like a colorist

At the end of the first stage, Raset has constructed the form with notable precision, using the dark red as a support for the picture's general color (see fig. 362, on the previous page). Just before he begins to paint, Roset enters into a kind of trance: Rapidly but confidently applying color, his hand dances in small circles, jumping from place to place, up and down. Back and forth he goes, attacking a point here, an area there, intuitively, concentrating only on the structure and the drawing, but at the same time resolving the color.

Raset suddenly stops working, goes over to his drawing box, and takes out a mirror. And just as Leonardo da Vinci recommended to his students, he studies the structure, dimensions, and proportions of his drawing in the mirror.

Raset then returns to his drawing, introducing new colors as he progresses. He applies them all sporadically, in specific areas: a little yellow here and there for the cushions, some more zig-zag strokes of red on the tights, and a slight touch of blue around the face (fig. 363). Raset then returns to the tights, this time to darken and shape them. He adds some red to the cheeks and a light flesh color to the thigh. Raset then shades the model's left arm with irregular strokes of light violet-purple, and does the same for the thigh. Now, using a piece of dark sienna chalk, he carefully emphasizes the contours of the arms, legs, and stomach. Raset explains ''With these contours I am recovering the drawing and its initial structure because it was beginning to blur beneath the colors'' (fig. 364). It is worth noting that in all of Raset's paintings the directions of the strokes are carefully planned so that they help to define the forms. The strokes used for the legs, arms, breasts, and thighs may be either diagonal or horizontal, but they are always cylindrical.

Figs. 363 to 365. The second stage. Raset begins to define the figure with several colors: the red of the tights, the highlights on the flesh with some subtle touches of yellow, the red of the shadows and the cheeks, and a few violet highlights to define the profile of the face. To end this session, Raset shades the lower right portion of the body with irregular strokes, creating a light purple mist that softens the drawing.

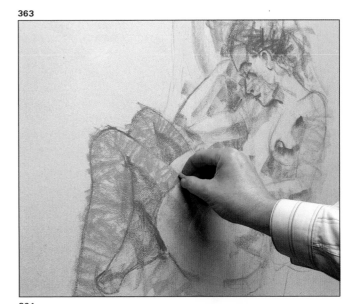

363

364

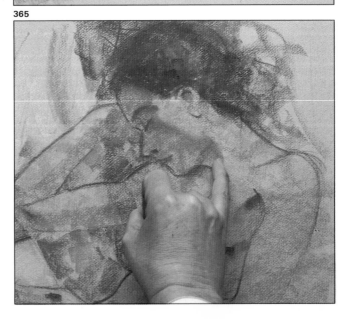

365

66

Now Raset concentrates on the color of the hair: He covers it with bold and resolute strokes that deliberately "cross the line" in order to leave a series of straight and round strokes around the head. Finally, he intensifies the color of the face, then blends it by softening it with his little finger (fig. 365).

As all good professionals do, Raset never focuses on just one part of the painting. He goes from one part to another, advancing the entire work in stages. As Ingres said, in this way the painting "is always finished in terms of each stage: project, sketch, advanced sketch..." Note that at the end of this second stage, the picture already suggests the color of the flesh, contrasts, light, and shadows. We could consider that the painting is practically "finished."

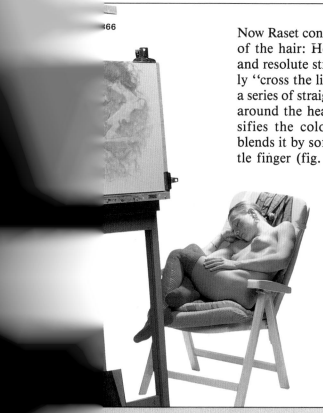

Figs. 366 and 367. Raset working from the model, and (below) the drawing/painting at the end of the second stage.

367

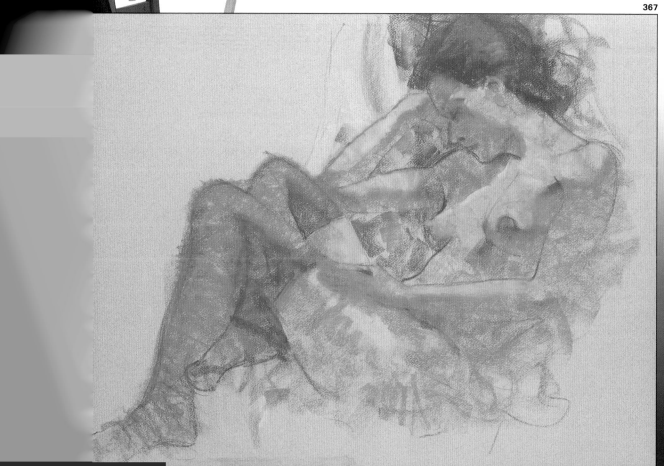

The last stage of Raset's drawing/painting

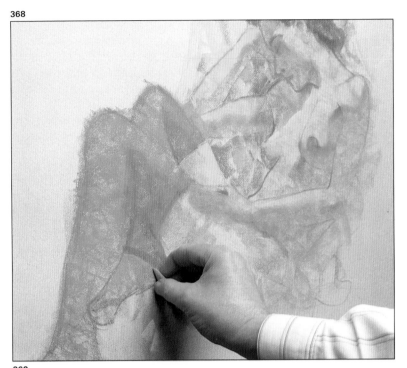

368

Up to this point, Raset has resolved lines, shadows, and gradations with direct strokes, without blending. Now he continues to draw and shape but finishes his work by blending it with his fingers and in some cases by using his forefinger covered with a cloth. "But you must be careful with the strokes and blending: They should never be so intense as to eliminate the paper's texture, especially in large areas."

Raset always holds a cloth in his left hand in order to clean his fingers, but on certain occasions, he paints with the color that is left on them.

With isolated, agitated strokes he paints the body's illuminated areas with an orangy-flesh color in order to create color contrast. He always considers the whole, never lingering over details. He constantly alternates painting with blending, occasionally using his cloth in order to soften color. This last procedure is generally used to correct color: When he decides that a particular area is too dark, he erases some of it with a cloth and then repaints it in a lighter color.

Raset is now accentuating the red of the tights. He uses this same color for the portions of the head in shadow and the right arm, thus creating a soft reflection. He goes on to paint spots of cerulean blue around the hair and profile. He now steps back to first look at the model, then the painting, then back at the model. "OK," he says, and signs it with a dedication: "To my friend Parramón, a great artist and master."

Note that Raset has totally ignored the lounge chair, the yellow cushion, and the blue towel. Here the artist has demonstrated his capacity for interpretation. Such elements would have disturbed the subject, *the female nude.* For this same reason he has decided from the beginning to leave unfinished the left arm and the con-

369

tours of the model's back and buttock. In this way he highlights the head, breasts, thighs, and legs, composing what Juan Raset set out to paint in pastel: an exquisite female figure.

370

Figs. 368 to 370. In the first of these figures Raset continues to intensify the values and colors of the previous stage. Figure 369 enables us to closely examine Raset's work. The finished work (fig. 370) is both a painting and a drawing.

The chromatic quality suits our subject—color—very well. Raset sums it all up: "Paint thinking about the color." And when it comes to the nude, Raset is a poet of the female body, painted—as Degas said—not by a man but by an artist.

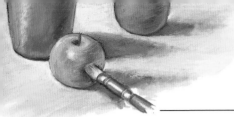

Paintings by José M. Parramón

I have been painting and exhibiting for a long time, and have written and published books on how to draw and paint for many years. My books have been translated into the twelve languages of the European Community as well as Japanese. Since almost all of my work has focused on teaching painting techniques, I paint in all media. I am also a perfectionist: Most of the works on this page have been painted at least twice, and I take great care to ensure that the composition, interpretation, and color of my paintings, as well as my books, will help to teach and encourage the reader to pick up a brush and paint.

371

372

373

376

375

378

377

Figs. 371 to 378. Watercolors are shown on page 150, and oils on 151. I have tried to bring together what I consider representative in terms of subject and media.

Parramón paints an urban landscape

379

Now you can see what I was talking about: I am going to paint this subject for the second time, although his time I will copy it from the reproduction that appears on page 8 of this book. I am not working from the painting in order to improve it, but only because the site itself no longer exists. The entrance to and the old quarter of "Baños de San Miguel" were demolished during the preparations for the 1992 Olympic Games in Barcelona. Of course, I might just as well paint another subject, but I have always found this one to be a good example of color, contrast, and complementaries.

I begin by sketching the subject with a piece of charcoal (fig. 379), and immediately determine the vanishing point (A), "directly in front of the observer, at eye level."

380

381

Fig. 379. I draw with charcoal, taking great care to situate the horizon line and vanishing point, where all perpendicular lines should converge. I fix the drawing...

Figs. 380 to 382. ...and begin to fill in spaces in order to cover the white of the canvas and avoid false contrasts. For the moment I am not worried about adjusting the colors to their maximum, since I will return to them later on to resolve tones and hues.

The first stage

Just to remind you again: In a parallel perspective such as this one, the vanishing point is found on the horizon line, bringing together all parallel lines perpendicular to that line. Perspective is essential, although you must not worry if it is not perfect. After all, we are not architects—we paint by eye, in the open air, not with a T-square, in a room with central heating and air conditioning.

I fix the charcoal with an aerosol fixative so that it won't mix with and dirty the oil paints, and then begin to paint.

First I fill in the spaces with the aim of neutralizing the white of the canvas. This should be done so as to avoid the effect of *simultaneous contrast* (a color appearing lighter or darker according to the color surrounding it). I paint the sky blue, though not exactly "blue," but a mix of Prussian blue and white, mixed with a touch of emerald green and a tiny bit of deep madder (fig. 380).

I continue to fill in the spaces: the houses on the left-hand side, the small yellow and white buildings in the background, the bluish shadow on the ground and the sign; I leave the windows and doors to work on later. At this point I have achieved the painting's general color scheme. Naturally it is not definitive, but it helps me to see the color contrasts (figs. 381 and 382).

It's important to note that the first stage (fig. 385) is not simply a series of *one-color uniform planes*. First I have painted the sky, the houses, the buildings, and the ground in one color each with a few variations, and then I have repainted them, adding some tones to diversify and enrich the color. In certain instances I have changed the color completely; the sky, for example, is now light blue.

Fig. 383. While filling in, I diversify and even modify the colors in certain ares. This enables me to get a general idea of the hues and thus work more comfortably.

382

383

The second stage: a general adjustment of color

384

385

386

387

388

389

Looking at the details of the painting on the opposite page, one might say that the second stage consists of adding final details. In figure 384 I have painted a ledge of the house in the middle ground. In the next image I start to paint the ironwork of the door in the background in ocher yellow, for which I use a flat, ox-hair No. 6 brush (fig. 385). The third reproduction shows how I erase part of the ground in shadow, which I then reconstruct after changing its form (fig. 386), which you can see in the finished painting below. I return to the ironwork, now yellow from the sunlight, in order to resolve it with a mix of medium yellow and a little vermilion. This mix yields what I call a "Kodak" yellow (fig. 387), and with it I reconstruct the "San Miguel" sign, moving the shadow a little over to the right. Before it coincid-

ed with the letter "U," and now it finishes with the "E" in diagonal, thus rectifying the error in perspective (fig. 388). In the last of these images you can see the construction of forms of the nearest building's top balcony, under the blind (fig. 389). In this second stage I have worked only on the forms and structures: the ledge, the ironwork, the shadow on the sign, the balcony, and so on. But don't get confused: Compare figures 390 and 383, which are the final steps of the first and second stages, and you will see that the basic difference between the two lies in the color adjustments. Look at the sky in figure 390: It is darker, and now is the definitive color of the painting. Also, the "Kodak" yellow of the second house is more intense, creating a bright complementary contrast with the dark blue sky. The

sienna-reddish color of the shadow of the second house is more concrete not only in form but also in color, with a bluish hue that contrasts with the part illuminated by the sun. The lateral plane in shadow of the second house is now more intense, accentuating a greenish tendency on the top floor and a bluish one on the bottom. I have also changed the color of the closest house, the bluish shadow on the sidewalk, and the bluish-green of the sign.

390

Figs. 384 to 390. Despite the fact that these images seem to be merely touched up, the truth is that in this second stage I am still developing the general color scheme. Check the final result on page 153 to see the series of changes and retouches of color on the sky, the ground, and the sidewalk.

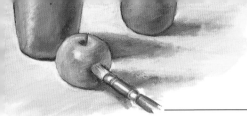

Final details and people

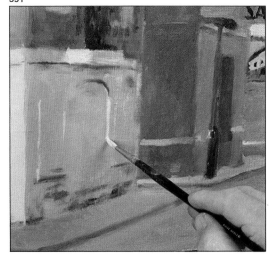

391

392

The painting is finished. I reality we could have said it was ready in the previous stage if it were not for one or two details, such as the inclusion of windows and false doors in the wall of the foreground (fig. 391) and the lines on the yellow and white walls of the building in the background (fig. 394), which I have drawn with the end of the brush. But there is one more factor: The picture lacks people. It would be inconceivable to paint an urban landscape without people. The painting at the end of the second stage looks more like an empty movie set without actors.

When including figures in an urban landscape such as this one, take care to paint all the heads at the same height, approximately at the horizon line, with those in the foreground a little higher and those in the background a little lower. They must be painted in a rougher manner, not too precisely. Use a No. 4 or 6 round brush. Make sure that what you are painting over is dry or the colors will become dirty.

The farther away and smaller the figures, the more orangy-red their flesh colors should be. The tone must be darker in the shadows and lighter in sunlight. Start with the head, then move on to the jacket or blouse and skirt or pants, then paint the arms and hair. When painting people, you should also take into account that when a figure is walking toward the viewer, we generally see one leg advancing while the other remains

393

394

395

Figs. 391 to 395. As the heading of this page indicates, this phase is dedicated to finishing a few final details and painting people, adding figures of people in the street. You should do this easily and spontaneously, painting over a dry canvas with clean colors, using a reddish orange for flesh tones, starting with the heads, all at the same height near the horizon line. Then add bodies, legs, and so on.

396

behind, half-hidden. If it is a woman in a skirt we see two knees and only one foot, forming a kind of elongated orangy-red triangle. If it is a man in trousers we see a longer triangle that goes from the hips to the feet.

And that is it. I hope you have found this book helpful in learning the theory and practice of color in painting.

Fig. 396. The finished work: This painting has a great deal of light and pronounced color contrasts. It could be called *fauvist* in its chromaticism and because it makes use of an evident interplay of blues and yellows.

Glossary

A

Abstract art. An art form that assumes that forms and colors have an intrinsic artistic value regardless of figurative representation. The Greek philosopher Plato anticipated this idea when, discussing the beauty of forms, he compared ''the living shapes of paintings'' with ''straight and curved lines or solid shapes obtained by the use of rulers and set squares,'' and remarked that ''the beauty of the latter is never relative as is the rest, but absolute and natural.''

Additive synthesis. White light is made up of six light colors. When these six colors are reflected by a white object, through *additive synthesis* we see the object as white.

Alla prima. From the Italian, ''at the first attempt''; executing a painting in a single session without any preparatory stages.

Atmosphere. A technique used to represent the third dimension, produced by varying intensities of contrast and color. This effect, also called *aerial perspective*, is emphasized when the subject or model is lit from the front.

Aurignac. A town in Haute-Garonne (France) in which fossilized bones dating back some 30,000 years were discovered in a cave in 1860. This discovery has since been dated to one of the sub-eras of the *paleolithic* period, when the first works of art were produced.

B

Binders. Liquid media that are mixed with ground pigments to produce oil or watercolor paints.

Black paintings. Murals painted in oil by Goya in a house located on the outskirts of Madrid, which he bought in 1819 and which

a critic called the ''Quinta del Sordo.'' In 1873, a German called Erlanger bought the house and in 1881 commissioned the artist Martínez Cubells to copy the murals onto canvas, which he then donated to the Prado Museum.

C

Chalk. A color medium that is similar to pastels but more stable and longer tasting. Cylindrical or square in shape and composed of pigment ground with oils, water, and gums, chalk is available in white, black, sienna, and blue.

Chiaroscuro. Those areas of a painting which, although they are in shadow, allow the subject to be seen. The technique of chiaroscuro can be defined as *the art of painting light in shadows*. Rembrandt was one of its great masters.

Colorism. A style of painting that essentially eliminates light and shadow to create volume, placing an emphasis on direct, frontal lighting and flat colors, in accordance with the ideas of Bonnard: ''Color can express *everything*, without volume or modeling.''

Complementary colors. Speaking in terms of *light colors*, complementary colors are secondary colors made from one primary and white light. For example, when yellow—made up of green and red—is added to blue, white light is recomposed. In terms of *pigment colors*, a complementary color is the contrasting or opposite color. For instance, the complementary of magenta is green.

Complementary colors, effect of. Related to simultaneous contrast and the phenomenon of successive images, the effect of complementary colors is produced by our

eyes which, when they see a certain color, will then see its complementary simultaneously.

Contrast. When two tones or colors differ considerably in value or intensity, contrast is produced. If the difference is great, such as that between white and black, or dark blue and yellow, the contrast can be sharp. When colors are similar, such as orange and red, the contrast is soft. Contrast results from a difference in *tone, color,* or *range,* or between *complementary colors,* as well as a result of *simultaneous contrast*.

D

Deer hair brush. A type of paint brush manufactured in Japan made from deer hair and bamboo. The tip of the brush is usually very wide and therefore ideal for painting watercolor washes over large backgrounds.

Dominant color. A musical term used in painting to express a dominant color or color range, for example, of *warm, cold,* or *neutral* colors.

F

Fauvism. Derived from the French word *fauve* (''beast''), this term was first used by a critic attending an exhibition held in 1905 in the Autumn Hall, Paris. The fauves or fauvists were headed by Matisse and also included Derain, Vlaminck, and others.

Frottage. Derived from the French verb *frotter* (to rub), a painting technique that consists of lightly loading the brush with thick paint and rubbing over an area that has already been painted and is dry or still slightly damp.

G

Glaze. A transparent layer of oil paint applied either as a first stage or on top of a color, which it then modifies.

Grisaille. A preparatory stage of oil painting which uses white, gray (with sienna, blue, and green), and black to compose the subject. Velázquez painted the first layer of his paintings in grisaille, over which he then drew and painted the subject.

H

Harmonization. Determining the correlation between one or more colors and another in order to produce a pleasing whole. These relationships are based on the *ranges of colors*, of which there are basically three: *warm, cold*, and *neutral*.

M

Mahl stick. In oil painting, a thin wooden stick topped by a small ball used for resting the hand to paint small details or areas, providing firm support and preventing the hand from touching the wet paint.

Mordiente. The stage of an oil painting when the paint is almost dry and a little sticky, but can still be worked on by dragging the brush over it.

N

Nanometer. A unit of measurement used to determine the length and frequency of electromagnetic waves. A nanometer is equivalent to one thousand millionth of a meter.

Naturalism. The aesthetic principle which states that nature and everything related to it are the only subjects of artistic worth. This term was probably first used by the art critics of the nineteenth century to refer to Coubert's work, and applied since then both to painting from that century and to classics from the Baroque and Renaissance periods, as well as to earlier artists such as Giotto, Cimabue, and Masaccio.